T0219471

DevOps with OpenShift
Cloud Deployments Made Easy

Stefano Picozzi, Mike Hepburn, and Noel O'Connor

Beijing · Boston · Farnham · Sebastopol · Tokyo 

DevOps with OpenShift

by Stefano Picozzi, Mike Hepburn, and Noel O'Connor

Printed in the United States of America.

Published by O'Reilly Media, Inc., 1005 Gravenstein Highway North, Sebastopol, CA 95472.

O'Reilly books may be purchased for educational, business, or sales promotional use. Online editions are also available for most titles (*http://oreilly.com/safari*). For more information, contact our corporate/institutional sales department: 800-998-9938 or *corporate@oreilly.com*.

Editors: Brian Anderson and Virginia Wilson	**Indexer:** Angela Howard
Production Editor: Nicholas Adams	**Interior Designer:** David Futato
Copyeditor: Jasmine Kwityn	**Cover Designer:** Randy Comer
Proofreader: Sonia Saruba	**Illustrator:** Rebecca Demarest

July 2017:   First Edition

Revision History for the First Edition
2017-07-07:   First Release

See *http://oreilly.com/catalog/errata.csp?isbn=9781491975961* for release details.

978-1-491-97596-1

[LSI]

Table of Contents

Preface

If you're old, don't try to change yourself, change your environment.

—B. F. Skinner

One view of DevOps is that it helps take on that last mile problem in software: value delivery. The premise is that encouraging behaviors such as teaming, feedback, and experimentation will be reinforced by desirable outcomes such as better software, delivered faster and at lower cost. For many, the DevOps discourse then quickly turns to automation. That makes sense as automation is an environmental intervention that is relatively actionable. If you want to change behavior, change the environment!

In this context, automation becomes a significant investment decision with strategic import. DevOps automation engineers face a number of design choices. What level of interface abstraction is appropriate for the automation tooling? Where should you separate automation concerns of an infrastructure nature from those that should be more application centric?

These questions matter because automation tooling that is accessible to all can better connect all the participants in the software delivery process. That is going to help foster all those positive teaming behaviors we are after. Automation that is decoupled from infrastructure provisioning events makes it possible to quickly tenant new project streams. Users can immediately self-serve without raising a new infrastructure requisition.

We want to open the innovation process to all, be they 10x programmers or citizen developers. Doing DevOps with OpenShift makes this possible, and this book will show you how.

This is a practical guide that will show how to easily implement and automate powerful cloud deployment patterns using OpenShift. The OpenShift container management platform provides a self-service platform for users. Its natively container-aware approach will allow us to show you an application-centric view to automation.

Who Should Read This Book

If you are keen to awaken your inner DevOps then this book is for you. It is intended for programmers who want to learn how to use OpenShift to automate the software delivery process to achieve continuous integration, delivery, and deployment.

Note that we deliberately take an application workload-centric view of the problem. Concerns related to the overall management and operation of the OpenShift *system* will be the subject of a forthcoming title in O'Reilly's OpenShift series.

We will step you through how to develop container-based applications that can be easily and safely changed via pipelines and powerful deployment patterns. Starting with a few simple steps to launch OpenShift as an all-in-one image on your workstation, we will cover examples for application environment configuration, persistent volume claims, and A/B, blue-green, and rolling or replacement deployment strategies. Techniques for third-party tool chain integration using webhooks will be explained and demonstrated.

This book builds on the material covered in *OpenShift for Developers* and so assumes some background knowledge of basic OpenShift development concepts such as:

- Developing and deploying an application.
- Using application templates.
- Managing application workloads.
- Working with Docker images.

As with the previous title, we also assume you are familiar with basic Linux or Windows shell commands, and how to install additional software on your computer. The software you install will provide you with a complete working OpenShift environment that you can use locally for development or testing.

We have used a PHP and a Node.js application for many of the examples in this book. You do not need to be proficient in PHP or Node.js. If you are familiar with any of the popular programming languages you will do just fine.

Why We Wrote This Book

As Red Hat consultants, we are often called upon to assist clients in the deployment and widespread adoption of OpenShift as their container management platform. They are drawn to OpenShift as a technology enabler for increased agility and responsiveness. In this context, change-ability can be the most critical of nonfunctional requirements. Continuous improvement needs continuous user feedback. We have found that the ability to push, test, and then roll forward or roll back small application changes to live users can become critical to realizing such benefits. In this book we want to help you implement DevOps practices using OpenShift so that you can quickly deliver quality applications that will make a difference for your users.

Online Resources

In this book you will install a self-contained OpenShift environment based on Open-Shift Origin (*https://www.openshift.org/*). This is the upstream open source version of OpenShift on which Red Hat's OpenShift Container Platform (*https://www.open shift.com/container-platform*), OpenShift Dedicated (*https://www.openshift.com/dedi cated/*), and OpenShift Online (*https://www.openshift.com/*) products are based.

Various options are available to stand up a self-contained environment. For this book, we will focus on the `oc cluster up` (*https://github.com/openshift/origin/blob/master/docs/cluster_up_down.md*) technique that starts up a local all-in-one cluster based on OpenShift Origin. Alternative approaches are available, such as the Vagrant all-in-one virtual machine described at the OpenShift Origin site (*https://www.openshift.org/vm/*). This procedure was covered in *OpenShift for Developers* and so is not repeated in detail here.

OpenShift Origin will always include all the latest features, with support being provided by the OpenShift community.

The OpenShift product releases are created as a regular snapshot of the OpenShift Origin project. The product releases do not always have the very latest features, but if you have a commercial Red Hat subscription, the product releases include support from Red Hat.

If you would like to try out the OpenShift Container Platform version, a couple of options are available.

The first is to register for a Red Hat Developers account (*http://develop ers.redhat.com/*). The Red Hat Developer Program allows you to access versions of Red Hat products for personal use on your own computer. One of the products made available through the program is the Red Hat Container Development Kit (*http://developers.redhat.com/products/cdk/overview/*). This includes a version of OpenShift that you can install on your own computer, but which is based on OpenShift Container Platform rather than OpenShift Origin.

A second way of trying out OpenShift Container Platform is via the Amazon Web Services (AWS) Test Drive program (*https://aws.amazon.com/testdrive/redhat/*). This will set you up an OpenShift environment running across a multinode cluster on AWS.

Take a look at more in-depth documentation on OpenShift and how to use it at the OpenShift documentation site (*https://docs.openshift.org/*).

Check out the OpenShift blog (*https://blog.openshift.com/*), where regular articles are published on OpenShift.

If you want to hear about how others in the OpenShift community are using Open-Shift, or wish to share your own experiences, you can join the OpenShift Commons (*http://commons.openshift.org/*).

If you have questions or issues, you can reach the OpenShift team through Stack Overflow (*http://stackoverflow.com/*), on Twitter (@openshift (*https://twitter.com/openshift*)), or in the #openshift channel on IRC's FreeNode network.

Conventions Used in This Book

The following typographical conventions are used in this book:

Italic
> Indicates new terms, URLs, email addresses, filenames, and file extensions.

`Constant width`
> Used for program listings, as well as within paragraphs to refer to program elements such as variable or function names, databases, data types, environment variables, statements, and keywords.

`Constant width bold`
> Shows commands or other text that should be typed literally by the user.

`Constant width italic`
> Shows text that should be replaced with user-supplied values or by values determined by context.

> This element signifies a tip or suggestion.

> This element signifies a general note.

> This element indicates a warning or caution.

Using Code Examples

Supplemental material (code examples, exercises, etc.) is available for download at *https://github.com/devops-with-openshift*.

This book is here to help you get your job done. In general, if example code is offered with this book, you may use it in your programs and documentation. You do not need to contact us for permission unless you're reproducing a significant portion of the code. For example, writing a program that uses several chunks of code from this book does not require permission. Selling or distributing a CD-ROM of examples from O'Reilly books does require permission. Answering a question by citing this book and quoting example code does not require permission. Incorporating a significant amount of example code from this book into your product's documentation does require permission.

We appreciate, but do not require, attribution. An attribution usually includes the title, author, publisher, and ISBN. For example: "*DevOps with OpenShift* by Stefano Picozzi, Mike Hepburn, and Noel O'Connor (O'Reilly). Copyright 2017 Red Hat, Inc., 978-1-491-97596-1."

If you feel your use of code examples falls outside fair use or the permission given above, feel free to contact us at *permissions@oreilly.com*.

O'Reilly Safari

Safari (formerly Safari Books Online) is a membership-based training and reference platform for enterprise, government, educators, and individuals.

Members have access to thousands of books, training videos, Learning Paths, interactive tutorials, and curated playlists from over 250 publishers, including O'Reilly Media, Harvard Business Review, Prentice Hall Professional, Addison-Wesley Professional, Microsoft Press, Sams, Que, Peachpit Press, Adobe, Focal Press, Cisco Press, John Wiley & Sons, Syngress, Morgan Kaufmann, IBM Redbooks, Packt, Adobe Press, FT Press, Apress, Manning, New Riders, McGraw-Hill, Jones & Bartlett, and Course Technology, among others.

For more information, please visit *http://oreilly.com/safari*.

How to Contact Us

Please address comments and questions concerning this book to the publisher:

O'Reilly Media, Inc.
1005 Gravenstein Highway North
Sebastopol, CA 95472
800-998-9938 (in the United States or Canada)
707-829-0515 (international or local)
707-829-0104 (fax)

To comment or ask technical questions about this book, send email to *bookquestions@oreilly.com*.

We have a web page for this book, where we list errata, examples, and any additional information. You can access this page at *http://bit.ly/devops_with_openshift*.

For more information about our books, courses, conferences, and news, see our website at *http://www.oreilly.com*.

Find us on Facebook: *http://facebook.com/oreilly*

Follow us on Twitter: *http://twitter.com/oreillymedia*

Watch us on YouTube: *http://www.youtube.com/oreillymedia*

Acknowledgments

Stefano

It's a privilege to contribute to a book such as this. For this, I am grateful to my family and Red Hat for allowing me to indulge in those private, quiet moments it takes to then get it done!

I also appreciate the many clients who have taken the time to share their aspirations and challenges with me. Software process improvement is hard. All the insights and suggestions presented here originate there.

Mike

One of my favorite quotes related to content creation is this one from Harry S. Truman: "It is amazing what you can accomplish if you do not care who gets the credit."

It is with this humility that I wish to acknowledge all of the fantastic work from the OpenShift community that has provided ideas that have gone into this book.

You Rock.

Noel

Writing this book has been a whole heap of fun and I'm grateful to Stefano and Mike for inviting me to participate in this project. I'd also like to thank my wife and children for their patience and support while writing this book.

The true power of this platform is in its open source foundations and the multitude of perspectives and opinions that only a diverse open community can bring. Thanks also to all those involved in the internal Red Hat teams who develop, productize, test, document, and support this platform.

## CHAPTER 1

Introduction to DevOps with OpenShift

This book provides a practical guide for using OpenShift as an enablement technology for DevOps. OpenShift's combination of container management platform with natively container-aware automation can bring those Developer and Operations constituencies together in ways not previously possible. This enables software work products to present themselves in a standardized form to your preferred continuous integration and delivery tool chains.

Container awareness makes it possible to leverage deployment strategies and quality of service characteristics honored by the container management platform and underlying orchestration engine. We can start thinking in terms of *containers-as-code* rather than *infrastructure-as-code*.

So to get started, let's review some key DevOps concepts as interpreted with a container-centric viewpoint.

DevOps

DevOps is concerned with aligning the constituents in the software delivery process to a common goal of value delivery—and it's not just Developers and Operators, but InfoSec and Quality Assurance functions and more. Recognize that wealth is created when the work product is valued by actors external to the production system. Value delivery outcomes are measured by metrics tied to production delivery velocity, quality, and waste. DevOps emphasizes behavioral- or cultural-related changes such as those which encourage teaming, inclusion, feedback, and experimentation. Technological interventions such as automation are central as they can reinforce such target behaviors. DevOps does not necessarily imply functional roles in software delivery such as development, quality assurance, or operations are merged or seconded. More important is that a professional respect and shared sensibility is formed across the delivery team.

Containers

Containers are the runtime representation of a packaging format based on a lightweight, immutable image. Runtime dependencies are resolved within the image which facilitates portability. This makes possible the agreement on a standardized software work product. Management and runtime tooling that is container aware can then be applied consistently no matter what the underlying technology stack. Container-based workloads are suitable for multi-tenancy on a single compute instance and when implemented securely can realize significant operation efficiencies. An important corollary is that launching a new workload does not incur the cost of provisioning new compute infrastructure. This enables a true on-demand, self-service experience for users.

Container Orchestration

Container orchestration involves the lifecycle management of container workloads, including functions such as to schedule, stop, start, and replicate across a cluster of machines. Compute resources for running workloads are abstracted, allowing the host infrastructure to be treated as a single logical deployment target. Kubernetes is an open source community project addressing container orchestration. It groups containers that make up an application into logical units for easy management and discovery, and features self-healing, service discovery, load balancing, and storage services among its rich feature set. Orchestration plays a critical role in our design goal of application-centricity as quality of service attributes and deployment patterns are executed by invoking Kubernetes API primitives.

Continuous Integration

Continuous integration (CI) concerns the integration of code from potentially multiple authors into a shared source code management (SCM) repository. Such check-ins could occur many times a day, and automation steps in such a process could include gates or controls to expose any issues as early as possible. SCMs such as Git include workflow support to commit to trunk, push, and merge code pull requests from multiple developers. With containers, a Git push event could be configured to then trigger an image build event via the webhooks mechanism.

Continuous Delivery

Once a CI strategy is in place, consideration can then move to achieving continuous delivery (CD). This involves automating the steps required to promote the work product from one environment to the next within the defined software development lifecycle (SDLC). Such steps could include automated testing, smoke, unit, functional, and static code analysis and static dependency checks for known security vulnerabilities. With containers, promotion in later stages of the SLC may merely involve the tagging of the (immutable) image to mark acceptance. Binary promotions are also possible such that only the image is pushed (to the target registry of the new environment), leaving source code in situ.

Continuous Deployment

By convention, we can denote the special case of automated continuous delivery to production as *continuous deployment* (CD). We make such a distinction because such deployments may be subject to additional governance processes and gates—for example, deliberate human intervention to manage risk and complete sign-off procedures. We make such a distinction because such deployments may be subject to additional governance processes. As per Figure 1-1, there may be scenarios for deliberate human intervention to manage risk and complete sign-off procedures.

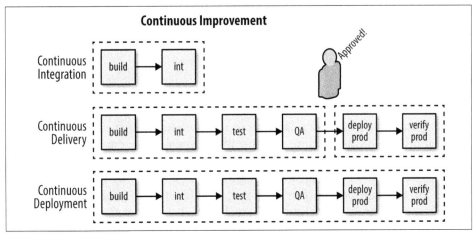

Figure 1-1. Continuous delivery versus deployment

Pipelines

Pipelines are a representation of the flow/automation in a CI/CD process. Typically a pipeline might call out discrete steps in the software delivery process and present them visually or via a high-level scripting language so the flow can be manipulated.

The steps might include build, unit tests, acceptance tests, packaging, documentation, reporting, and deployment and verification phases. Well-designed pipelines help deliver better quality code faster by enabling participants in the software delivery process to more easily diagnose and respond to feedback. As illustrated in Figure 1-2, diagnosis and response turnaround can be accelerated by organizing releases into smaller and more frequent release bundles.

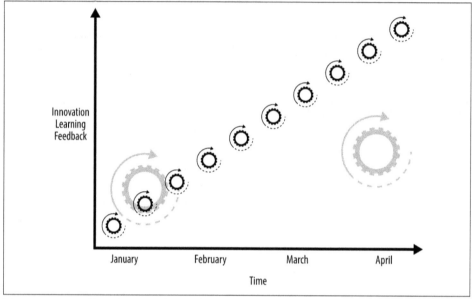

Figure 1-2. Smaller releases, release often, faster feedback

Software Configuration Management

For our purposes we will take a narrower view of software configuration management (CM) and focus on the recommended software engineering practice of separating dynamic configuration from static runtime software. Doing so allows developers and operations engineers to change the configuration without having to rebuild the runtime such as might occur when deploying to different environments. Containers, based as they are on immutable images, amplify this behavior as the alternative would be configuration layered across multiple images for each deployment scenario.

Deployment Patterns

Aligned with the goal of automation across all steps in the software delivery lifecycle are patterns for deployment. We look here for strategies that can balance across criteria including safety, testability, reversibility, and downtime minimization in cloud-scale scenarios. Some deployment patterns also offer opportunities for capturing and responding to feedback. An A/B deployment allows for testing a user-defined hypothesis such as whether application version A is more effective than B. Usage results can then drive weighted load balancing across the alternatives. Automation of deployment strategies in this DevOps world are implemented by driving the orchestration APIs.

Continuous Improvement

Let's conclude this chapter by covering continuous improvement (Figure 1-3), which should be the thread that connects all of the process improvement–related practices summarized. The environment changes and so must we. These practices make it easy and inexpensive to experiment, formulate, and test hypotheses, as well as capture, act on, and experiment with the feedback received. This way we can continue to inject energy into the system and so maintain a state of dynamic stability—a balance of adaptive/agile versus fixed/stable.

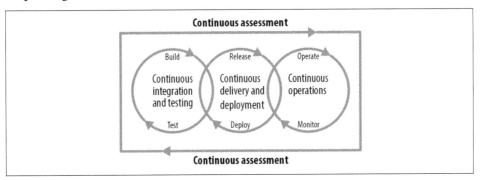

Figure 1-3. Continuous improvement

Summary

We covered here some of what is unique and nuanced about DevOps with OpenShift and why it matters. Realizing these DevOps concepts using natively container-aware automation can bring cloud deployment power to *all* the people, from 10x programmer to citizen developer. The following chapters will show you how.

## CHAPTER 2

Installing the All-In-One OpenShift

The same OpenShift codebase can take on many form factors. It can be a large public cloud deployment, offered as a managed service, a private instance in your company's data center, or as small as a local installation on your own workstation. This makes for a very convenient platform for evaluating, learning, and testing OpenShift-based workloads. Skills developed on a local instance are transferable to more complex distributed topologies.

The easiest way to get started is to visit the OpenShift website (*https://www.open shift.com*) and register for a free developer account. This will suffice for many of the examples covered in this book. Once registered, you can log in and you are good to go!

Another option is to use a local OpenShift all-in-one cluster on your own workstation. This is a fully functioning OpenShift instance with an integrated Docker registry, OpenShift master, and node. It can support both the upstream OpenShift Origin and OpenShift Container Platform versions. The aim of this feature is to allow web developers and other interested parties to run OpenShift V3 on their own computer. The cluster will be routable from your local system so you can treat it like a hosted version of OpenShift and can view the URLs you create.

As your own private instance, you can create as many projects as you like, push and pull to your registry, create local persistent volumes, and have cluster admin access. Here we will document building this using the oc cluster up command.

Software Requirements

The oc cluster up command starts a local OpenShift all-in-one cluster with a configured registry, router, image streams, and default templates. By default, the command requires a working Docker connection. However, if running in an environment with Docker Machine installed, it can create a Docker machine for you.

The oc cluster up command will create a default user and project, and once it completes will allow you to start using the command line to create and deploy apps with commands like oc new-app, oc new-build, and oc run. It will also print out a URL to access the management console for your cluster.

So let's get started. We are going to install the latest OpenShift client tools, install Docker, and then start a local cluster instance.

 The all-in-one cluster uses xip.io to provide DNS resolution with application URLs. The advantage of this is that you actually get routable URLs to your local machine without browser or separate DNS configuration steps. The drawback is that you need to be online whenever you use the cluster and xip.io may be blocked by your company's firewalls. Verify xip.io accessibility using a command such as nslookup and check that it can return an address in the non-authoritative answer section:

```
$ nslookup x.127.0.0.1.xip.io
Server:        61.9.195.193
Address:       61.9.195.193#53

Non-authoritative answer:
Name:   x.127.0.0.1.xip.io
Address: 127.0.0.1
```

Install OpenShift oc Client Tools

OpenShift 3 allows you to work using a command-line interface (CLI), web console, or via the Eclipse IDE using the latest JBoss tools. The CLI tool is known as oc and is what we will use in most cases. It's a single Go executable, so installation is simply a matter of downloading the tool and adding it to your PATH. Choose the latest, stable release from *https://github.com/openshift/origin/releases*, select the download that matches your operating system environment, update your PATH, and you are good to go.

For example, if I extracted the contents to the CLI directory in my home directory, I would issue the following command in both Linux and macOS to update the PATH and then verify success:

```
$ export PATH=$PATH:~/cli/

$ oc version
oc v1.4.1+3f9807a
kubernetes v1.4.0+776c994
features: Basic-Auth
```

```
Server https://127.0.0.1:8443
openshift v1.4.0-rc1+b4e0954
kubernetes v1.4.0+776c994
```

 What version of OpenShift is that? The output from the `oc version` command indicates that we have downloaded v1.4.1 of the OpenShift Origin client tools. This means that when we come to launch our local instance using `oc cluster up`, v1.4.1 of OpenShift Origin distribution will be pulled down.

For Windows users, the specific details for updating your PATH varies slightly between releases. Using Windows 10, right-click the bottom lefthand corner to raise the Power User task menu, then click System, Advanced System Settings, and finally, select Environment Variables. Once the dialog opens, select the Path variable and add ";C:\CLI" at the end (ensure you replace "C:\CLI" with the location of where you extracted the tool). You could also just copy it to *C:\Windows* or a directory you know is already on your path.

Install Docker

The `oc cluster up` command looks for a working Docker connection. The installation and configuration instructions for Linux, macOS, and Windows environments are covered in the documentation website for Local Cluster Management (*https://github.com/openshift/origin/blob/master/docs/cluster_up_down.md*). Refer to the website for configuration instructions for your environment, but take note of the requirement to configure for an insecure registry parameter of 172.30.0.0/16 in each case. If using Docker for Mac or Docker for Windows, you configure this setting from the Preferences GUI. Once installed, verify Docker is functioning before proceeding. For this book, Docker version 1.13.0 was used. Note that if you will be attempting more memory-intensive use cases, increase the assigned memory for Docker:

```
$ docker version
Client:
 Version:      1.13.0
 API version:  1.25
 ...

$ docker run hello-world
Unable to find image 'hello-world:latest' locally
latest: Pulling from library/hello-world
78445dd45222: Pull complete
Digest: sha256:c5515758d4c5e1e838e9cd307f6c6a0d620b5e07e6f927b07d05f6d12a1ac8d7
Status: Downloaded newer image for hello-world:latest
```

```
Hello from Docker!
This message shows that your installation appears to be working correctly.
...
```

 Docker for Windows is available for Windows 10 and Windows Server 2016. If you are running earlier versions, then go for the Vagrant self-contained OpenShift (*https://www.openshift.org/vm/*).

Launch OpenShift

With Docker and the oc tools installed and verified, we are ready to launch Open-Shift! The oc cluster command accepts various switches, but two we will take special note of are the host-data-dir and host-config-dir parameters. These allow you to specify a location for storing OpenShift cluster system state. Doing so enables you to set up named "profiles" for separate cluster instances within the same workstation that you can return to later. For the first invocation do something like below, replacing $HOME to reflect your environment and $PROFILE to, for example, "DevOps-WithOpenShift". This first attempt may take a few minutes as it downloads the Open-Shift distribution. Make note of the URL for the server as we will be referring to that later.

```
$ oc cluster up \
    --host-data-dir='$HOME/oc/profiles/$PROFILE/data' \
    --host-config-dir='$HOME/oc/profiles/$PROFILE/config'

-- Checking OpenShift client ... OK
-- Checking Docker client ... OK
-- Checking Docker version ... OK
-- Checking for existing OpenShift container ... OK
-- Checking for openshift/origin:v1.4.1 image ...
   Pulling image openshift/origin:v1.4.1
   Pulled 1/3 layers, 41% complete
   Pulled 2/3 layers, 76% complete
   Pulled 3/3 layers, 100% complete
   Extracting
   Image pull complete
...
-- Server Information ...
   OpenShift server started.
   The server is accessible via web console at:
       https://192.168.99.100:8443

   You are logged in as:
       User:     developer
       Password: developer
```

```
To login as administrator:
    oc login -u system:admin
```

The *profile* feature described is available when using a native Docker service (e.g., Docker for Mac or Docker for Windows). Environments using Docker Toolbox would pass the `--create-machine` switch instead at first-time launch in order to create a Docker virtual machine driver.

 By default, `oc cluster up` will pull down from the upstream OpenShift Origin repository, v1.4.1 in this case. To point to a specific enterprise image, and version, add the `--image` and `--version` switches to the cluster up invocation. For example, adding `--image=registry.access.redhat.com/openshift3/ose` and `--version=v3.4` will launch using OpenShift Container Platform V3.4.

 Windows users can launch the equivalent instruction on Power-Shell, albeit using the ^ character for command-line continuation. Linux and macOS users can also consider passing an additional parameter `--public-hostname=127.0.0.1` to ensure an OpenShift server on 127.0.0.1:8443.

Now let's restart the OpenShift cluster using the `use-existing-config` parameter and point to the saved named profile:

```
$ oc cluster down

$ oc cluster up \
    --host-data-dir='$HOME/oc/profiles/$PROFILE/data' \
    --host-config-dir='$HOME/oc/profiles/$PROFILE/config' \
    --use-existing-config

...
```

 The `oc cluster` command supports many switches. There are various open source projects that have built convenience wrappers and tools to simplfy usage. Some of these include Minishift (*https:// github.com/minishift/minishift*) and oc-cluster-wrapper (*https:// github.com/openshift-evangelists/oc-cluster-wrapper*).

Verify Your Environment

Let's now check that we are good to go by logging in using the CLI. We will then verify our installation by creating an application.

Log In Using the Command Line

```
$ oc login -u developer -p developer
Login successful.

You have one project on this server: "myproject"

Using project "myproject".

$ oc project myproject
Already on project "myproject" on server "https://127.0.0.1:8443".

$ oc new-app --name='cotd' --labels name='cotd' php~https://github.com/devops-
with-openshift/cotd.git -e SELECTOR=cats
--> Found image 1875070 (10 days old) in image stream "openshift/php" under tag
"5.6" for "php"

    Apache 2.4 with PHP 5.6
    -----------------------
    Platform for building and running PHP 5.6 applications

    Tags: builder, php, php56, rh-php56

    * A source build using source code from https://github.com/devops-with-
openshift/cotd.git will be created
        * The resulting image will be pushed to image stream "cotd:latest"
        * Use 'start-build' to trigger a new build
    * This image will be deployed in deployment config "cotd"
    * Port 8080/tcp will be load balanced by service "cotd"
        * Other containers can access this service through the hostname "cotd"

--> Creating resources with label name=cotd ...
    imagestream "cotd" created
    buildconfig "cotd" created
    deploymentconfig "cotd" created
    service "cotd" created
--> Success
    Build scheduled, use 'oc logs -f bc/cotd' to track its progress.
    Run 'oc status' to view your app.

$ oc expose service cotd
route "cotd" exposed
```

 Windows users with Docker for Windows installed should invoke the `cluster up` and `cluster down` command from PowerShell. Some of the labs to follow may describe Linux/Bash-style command-line operations. Windows users can reproduce such instructions using Bash for Windows or an equivalent.

Log In from Console

The console can be accessed using the OpenShift server console URL as displayed during the launch output (*https://127.0.0.1:8443/console/*). Log in using "developer" as the username and "developer" as the password. Then visit "My Project" to check the application you just created using the CLI (Figure 2-1).

Figure 2-1. My project with COTD application

Click the route link as displayed in your console—for example, *http://cotd-myproject. 127.0.0.1.xip.io*. If all is functioning correctly you should see something like Figure 2-2.

 While you are test-driving your brand-new, all-in-one cluster, why not check out the profile feature? Just shut down your running cluster and restart using a different profile name. Then toggle between the different profiles to verify system state is preserved within each profile, and restart. System configuration for each profile will be located as specified in your `--host-data-dir` and `--host-config-dir` launch runtime switches.

Figure 2-2. Cats!

Working with Storage

For some of the labs to follow you may wish to attach storage to your container running in your local cluster instance. The approach described is valid for a cluster instance launched using a native Docker service (i.e., not using the --create-machine switch). To do so using the oc CLI, follow these steps:

1. Create a persistent volume (pv).
2. Set up the volume claim and assign to a deploymentConfig.

Create a Persistent Volume

To create a persistent volume (pv), you need to log in as the cluster admin user and issue the following instruction, replacing $VOLUMENAME, $VOLUMESIZE, and $VOLUME PATH to reflect your environment—for example, sample settings could be myvolume, 1Gi, and /tmp/myvolume (a complete review of available configuration options can be found in the documentation (*http://red.ht/2nc8KYx*)):

```
$ oc login -u system:admin

$ oc create -f -  << EOF!
apiVersion: v1
kind: PersistentVolume
metadata:
  name: $VOLUMENAME
spec:
  capacity:
    storage: $VOLUMESIZE
  accessModes:
    - ReadWriteOnce
    - ReadWriteMany
  persistentVolumeReclaimPolicy: Recycle
  hostPath:
    path: $VOLUMEPATH
EOF!
persistentvolume "myvolume" created
```

The host path ($VOLUMEPATH) needs to be shared to Docker and expressed using a POSIX-style path convention. If using Docker for Mac or Docker for Windows, visit the Docker Preferences to update the sharing settings. In Windows, $VOLUMEPATH would take the form C/path/to/directory.

You may be wondering what those "access modes" are. The Kubernetes documentation (*http://bit.ly/2oDjyz5*) summarizes this as RWO (ReadWriteOnce), the volume can be mounted as read-write by a single node; ROX (ReadOnlyMany), the volume can be mounted read-only by many nodes; and RWX (ReadWriteMany), the volume can be mounted as read-write by many nodes.

Set Up the Volume Claim

You can create a persistent volume claim (PVC) and assign it to a `deploymentConfig` in a single operation using the `oc volume`. Assuming you have created an application called "cotd" inside project "myproject", then you would issue an instruction similar to below. Replace $VOLUMECLAIMNAME, $VOLUMECLAIMSIZE, $MOUNTPATH, and $VOLUME NAME to reflect your environment. Sample settings could be `myvolumeclaim`, `100Mi`, and `/opt/app-root/src/data`. Note that in this instance, the $MOUNTPATH denotes the path inside your container:

```
$ oc login -u developer -p developer

$ oc project myproject

$ oc volume dc/cotd --add \
  --name=images
```

```
      --type=persistentVolumeClaim \
      --mount-path=/opt/app-root/src/data/images \
      --claim-name=$VOLUMECLAIMNAME \
      --claim-size=$VOLUMECLAIMSIZE \
      --mount-path=$MOUNTPATH \
      --containers=cotd \
      --overwrite
persistentvolumeclaims/myvolumeclaim
deploymentconfig "cotd" updated
```

 Creating a PVC and attaching that claim to your deployment configuration can also be completed using the OpenShift Console. For PVC creation, look for the "Storage" option in the left margin of the Project menu. Similarly, "Attach Storage" can be found in the Actions drop-down list, accessible from the Applications → "Deployments left-margin" menu option.

Create a GitHub Account

Similar to the approach taken with *OpenShift for Developers*, you will be cloning and forking Git repositories for some of the labs in this book. If you don't have one already, go and create a GitHub account at *https://github.com*.

Alternative Form Factors

As noted, the same OpenShift codebase can take on many form factors. We have spent some time here describing an `oc cluster up` setup. This offers the convenience of a local instance you own and control including `system:admin` cluster authority. Project resources are only as limited by your own system capacity. We also mentioned other local installation types you might wish to explore such as Minishift (*https://github.com/minishift/minishift*). In either case, given its focus on application developers, these OpenShift installation types should *not* be used in production. You can also experiment with other options such as installing your own OpenShift cluster as described at the documentation site (*https://docs.openshift.com*). And for those exercises not requiring OpenShift administration access, you are encouraged to register and avail yourself of the OpenShift Online (V3) (*https://www.openshift.com*) Cloud service which provides a running, ready-to-use development platform.

Summary

In this chapter, we set up your local machine so you have a working instance of OpenShift running and ready to interact with. We have focused on the `oc cluster up` technique, but you are welcome to use any of the alternatives mentioned. You are going to find the profile feature very handy as you play around with the labs to come. So now it's ready, set, code!

## CHAPTER 3

Deployments

A completely automated deployment process is a must in modern software environments. The time between when software is written and tested till it is deployed into production (so it can realize its business value) makes up a software delivery lifecycle that should be as quick and smooth as your organizational processes will allow.

This ability to rapidly deploy software into production safely is behind the continuous delivery movement. Minimizing downtime while this software change occurs is a key concern. In this chapter you are going to learn some of the common approaches to deployment using OpenShift.

The Replication Controller

A deployment in OpenShift is a *replication controller* based on a user-defined template called a *deployment configuration*. Deployments are created manually or in response to triggered events. OpenShift provides:

- A deployment configuration, which is a template for deployments
- *Triggers* that drive automated deployments in response to events
- User-customizable strategies to transition from the previous deployment to the new deployment
- Rollback to a previous deployment
- Replication scaling (manual and automated)

If you don't think you need any of these deployment benefits, you can always spin up a replication controller or pod definition on OpenShift without having a deployment configuration at all.

Deployment Strategies

OpenShift provides deployment strategies that are defined by each deployment configuration. Each application will have its own requirements for availability and quality of service during a deployment. Architectural consideration should be made at design and development time for applications to take into account state (e.g., session state, atomic data—that is, what is the source of truth) and its effects on the quality of business service during updates to the application. For example, an application server that clusters server-side session state will have different concerns than a stateless application that relies on client-side caching only.

OpenShift provides strategies to support a variety of deployment scenarios, which we will cover in the following sections.

Rolling

The *rolling* strategy is the default strategy used if no strategy is specified on a deployment configuration. The rolling strategy performs a rolling update and supports *lifecycle hooks* for injecting code into the deployment process.

The rolling strategy will:

- Execute any *pre* lifecycle hook
- Scale up the new deployment based on the surge configuration
- Scale down the old deployment based on the max unavailable configuration
- Repeat this scaling until the new deployment has reached the desired replica count and the old deployment has been scaled to zero
- Execute any *post* lifecycle hook

When scaling down, the rolling strategy waits for pods to become ready so it can decide whether further scaling would affect availability. If scaled-up pods never become ready, the deployment will eventually time out and result in a deployment failure.

Let's try this out using our welcome busybox image example. When using oc new-app against a Docker image, OpenShift will create a deployment configuration of type *rolling* by default:

```
$ oc login -u developer -p developer
$ oc new-project welcome --display-name="Welcome" --description="Welcome"
$ oc new-app devopswithopenshift/welcome:latest --name=myapp
$ oc set probe dc myapp --readiness --open-tcp=8080 \
    --initial-delay-seconds=5 --timeout-seconds=5
$ oc set probe dc myapp --liveness -- echo ok
$ oc expose svc myapp --name=welcome
```

If we look at the deployment configuration we can see the rolling deployment strategy as well as the other details about the deployment:

```
$ oc describe dc myapp
...
Replicas:      1
Triggers:      Config, Image(myapp@latest, auto=true)
Strategy:      Rolling
...
```

Triggers

Two triggers were added to our deployment: a ConfigChange and ImageChange trigger. This means that every time we update the deployment configuration or deploy a new image, an event is generated that triggers a new deployment.

If a ConfigChange trigger is defined on a deployment configuration, the first *replication controller* is created soon after the deployment configuration itself. If *no* triggers are defined on a deployment configuration, a manual deployment will be needed. We can manually trigger our deployment in the web-ui or by typing:

```
$ oc deploy myapp --latest
```

If we watch the deployment in the web-ui, we can see that the old pod is not stopped and removed until the new pod deployment has successfully passed our defined *liveness* and *readiness* health check probes. It is crucial for correct deployment behavior that we set them appropriately for each application (Figure 3-1).

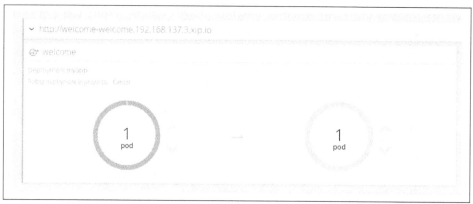

Figure 3-1. Rolling strategy on deployment

We can test the HTTP response of our application during a deployment, which should show all HTTP 200 OK responses while our deployment runs. In a separate shell, run the following command (replace the welcome route URL/IP address to suit your environment):

```
$ while true; do curl -I http://welcome-welcome.192.168.137.3.xip.io/ \
    2>/dev/null | head -n 1 | cut -d$' ' -f2; sleep 1; done
200
200
...
```

It is also possible to cancel and retry deployments using the cancel and retry flags (see `oc deploy -h` for details). To see the triggers on any deployment configuration, the following commands can be used:

```
$ oc set triggers dc myapp
NAME                       TYPE    VALUE                 AUTO
deploymentconfigs/myapp    config                        true
deploymentconfigs/myapp    image   myapp:latest (myapp)  true
```

We can easily manipulate triggers through the command-line interface. We can turn off all the triggers:

```
$ oc set triggers dc myapp --remove-all
```

The terminology is a bit confusing, because the config trigger is still there, just disabled (the AUTO flag is set to *false*). The image-based trigger has been removed.

```
$ oc set triggers dc myapp
NAME                       TYPE    VALUE  AUTO
deploymentconfigs/myapp    config          false
```

We could also have disabled just the config change trigger by itself:

```
$ oc set triggers dc myapp --from-config --remove
```

Let's re-enable just the config change trigger:

```
$ oc set triggers dc myapp --from-config
```

We can create triggers from *image change* events so that if a new image stream becomes available we can trigger a new deployment. Let's create an image change trigger for the base *busybox* image stream and add back our myapp ImageChange trigger we removed earlier:

```
# import image stream into our namespace
$ oc import-image docker.io/busybox:latest --confirm

# Add an image trigger to a deployment config
$ oc set triggers dc myapp --from-image=welcome/busybox:latest \
    --containers=myapp

# Add our myapp image trigger back as well
$ oc set triggers dc myapp --from-image=welcome/myapp:latest \
    --containers=myapp

$ oc set triggers dc myapp
NAME                        TYPE     VALUE                   AUTO
deploymentconfigs/myapp     config                           true
deploymentconfigs/myapp     image    busybox:latest (myapp)  true
deploymentconfigs/myapp     image    myapp:latest (myapp)    true
```

Recreate

The *Recreate* strategy has basic rollout behavior and supports lifecycle hooks for injecting code into the deployment process.

The Recreate strategy will:

- Execute any *pre* lifecycle hook
- Scale down the previous deployment to zero
- Execute any *mid* lifecycle hook
- Scale up the new deployment
- Execute any *post* lifecycle hook

Using the previous example, we can change the strategy from its default to a Recreate strategy using the patch command:

```
$ oc delete project welcome
$ oc new-project welcome --display-name="Welcome" --description="Welcome"
$ oc new-app devopswithopenshift/welcome:latest --name=myapp
$ oc patch dc myapp -p '{"spec":{"strategy":{"type":"Recreate"}}}'
$ oc set probe dc myapp --readiness --open-tcp=8080 \
    --initial-delay-seconds=5 --timeout-seconds=5
```

```
$ oc set probe dc myapp --liveness -- echo ok
$ oc expose svc myapp --name=welcome
```

If we force a new deployment:

```
$ oc deploy myapp --latest
```

The old pod is scaled down, and a new pod deployment proceeds.

Custom

The Custom strategy allows you to provide your own deployment behavior. This could be based on a custom image and configuration that you define. The replica count of the new deployment will initially be zero. The responsibility of the strategy is to make the new deployment active using the logic that best serves the needs of the user.

There isn't any custom deployment behavior, but this is how you might invoke such behavior—overriding the deployment image, command, and argument, for example:

```
$ oc patch dc myapp \
    -p '{"spec":{"strategy":{"type":"Custom",
    "customParams":{"image":"devopswithopenshift/welcome:latest",
    "command":["/bin/echo","a custom deployment command argument"]}}}}'
```

In this case we simply call */bin/echo*, which exists with a zero success status on deployment. The documentation (*http://red.ht/2p2FoIo*) for this strategy provides further information.

Lifecycle Hooks

The recreate and rolling strategies support lifecycle hooks that allow behavior to be injected into the deployment process at predefined points within the strategy. We are going to use OpenShift *pre-* and *post-* exec hooks in a worked example.

Hooks have a type-specific field that describes how to execute the hook. Currently, *pod-based* hooks are the only supported hook type, specified by the execNewPod field.

- The *pre-deployment* hook is executed just before the new image is deployed.
- The *mid-deployment* hook (Recreate strategy only) is executed after all instances of your old image are shut down.
- The *post-deployment* hook is executed just after the new image is deployed.

OpenShift will spin-up an *extra* instance of your built image, execute your hook script(s), and then shut the instance down.

Database Example

Persistent volumes (PVs) are used in this example. We touched on these in Chapter 2. If the persistent volume claims (PVCs) that get created are not *Bound*, check the STATUS by calling `oc get pvc`.

Ensure you have created PVs and check that the `AccessMode` of your PVC matches the PV (e.g., RWO, RWX). If you are not familiar with persistent volumes, check out the documentation (*http://red.ht/2obwqeK*).

Generally speaking, the rolling deployment strategy should not be used with databases. Generally, database corruption could occur if two instances of the database are running at the same time on the same database files.

The use of RWX volumes should always be used with a rolling deployment strategy; otherwise, multipod, multinode deployments may fail.

In the example that follows, we are going to create a Postgres database schema and load the default data using Liquibase (*http://www.liquibase.org/bestpractices.html*) change sets. If you haven't come across this library before, there are alternative database migration libraries such as Flyway (*https://github.com/flyway*) that may be familiar.

We use two containers in the example:

- The database configuration is supplied by the *dbinit* container. Configuration (via liquibase) is layered into the Docker image at */deployments*. The change set records are exported to an XML file on a PVC as the last (post- hook) step.

- A *Postgres database* container.

By using two containers we can keep the database runtime and its configuration separate. Liquibase change sets allow the example to be rerun multiple times as the same change set will not be applied twice. Another spin on this example is to execute a pre lifecycle hook to initialize the database and a mid lifecycle hook to perform the database schema changes.

The example creates a schema called *test* in a Postgres database. The schema generation uses annotated SQL scripts for data loading. The deployment hooks commands are specified in the JSON template file. If you examine the template file, you will see that the Postgres database connection for Liquibase is specified using environment variables.

Create a Postgres database on OpenShift using a *template* and set a Recreate deployment strategy:

```
$ oc new-project postgres --display-name="postgres" --description="postgres"
$ oc create -f https://raw.githubusercontent.com/openshift/openshift-ansible/
master/roles/openshift_examples/files/examples/v1.4/db-templates/postgresql-
persistent-template.json
$ oc new-app --template=postgresql-persistent \
    -p POSTGRESQL_USER=user \
    -p POSTGRESQL_PASSWORD=password \
    -p POSTGRESQL_DATABASE=test
$ oc patch dc postgresql -p '{"spec":{"strategy":{"type":"Recreate"}}}'
$ oc set env dc postgresql POSTGRESQL_ADMIN_PASSWORD=password
```

Once deployed and running, you should see output similar to:

```
$ oc get pods
NAME                    READY    STATUS    RESTARTS   AGE
postgresql-2-o662j      1/1      Running   0          5m
```

Log in to the *test* database as follows:

```
$ oc rsh $(oc get pods -lapp=postgresql-persistent -o name)
$ psql -h localhost -d test -U postgres
psql (9.5.4)
Type "help" for help.
test=#
```

Using Postgres commands, let's show tables \dt+ and list schemas \dn. You should see
the following:

```
test=# \dt+
No relations found.

test=# \dn
  List of schemas
  Name  |  Owner
--------+----------
 public | postgres
(1 row)
```

Enter Ctrl-D, Ctrl-D (or type **\q, exit**) to quit.

We are going to use an application template to create the database initializer pod that
uses Liquibase change sets.

> See the product documentation on application templates and how
> you create them at *http://red.ht/2nYVBil*.

The schema creation and data load occur in the deployment pre-hook. We generate
an XML representation of the changelog table using the post-deployment hook and
store that on a persistent volume:

```
$ oc create -f https://raw.githubusercontent.com/devops-with-openshift/
liquibase-example/master/dbinit-data-pvc.yaml
$ oc new-app --name=dbinit --strategy=docker \
    https://github.com/devops-with-openshift/liquibase-example.git
# we delete the generated deployment config
$ oc delete dc dbinit
# and recreate our deployment config with our own hooks defined
$ oc process \
    -f https://raw.githubusercontent.com/devops-with-openshift/liquibase-
example/master/dbinit-deployment-config.json \
    -v="IMAGE_STREAM=$(oc export is dbinit --template='{{range .spec.tags}}
{{.from.name}}{{end}}')" \
    | oc create -f -
# trigger a deployment
$ oc deploy dbinit --latest
```

You may track the progress using:

```
$ oc logs -f dc dbinit
--> pre: Running hook pod ...
DEBUG 2/2/17 10:33 AM: liquibase: Connected to user@jdbc:postgresql://
172.30.161.12:5432/test
...
```

Once the dbinit pod runs, you should see successful *Monitoring* events for the
deployment hooks when the db-init pod starts:

```
$ oc get events | grep dbinit
...
8:26:23 AM      dbinit Deployment Config      Normal   Started   Running pre-
hook ("sh -c cd /deployments && ./liquibase --defaultSchemaName=public --
url=jdbc:postgresql://${POSTGRESQL_SERVICE_HOST:-127.0.0.1}:5432/test --
driver=org.postgresql.Driver update -Dauthor=mike -Dschema=MY_SCHEMA") for
deployment postgres/dbinit-1
...
8:26:47 AM      dbinit Deployment Config      Normal   Started   Running post-
hook ("sh -c rm -f /data/baseline.xml && cd /deployments && ./liquibase --
defaultSchemaName=my_schema --changeLogFile=/data/baseline.xml --
url=jdbc:postgresql://${POSTGRESQL_SERVICE_HOST:-127.0.0.1}:5432/test --
driver=org.postgresql.Driver generateChangeLog") for deployment postgres/
dbinit-1
...
```

From the database login shell, we can also see tables and data created in the database
itself:

```
test=# \dt+
                          List of relations
 Schema |          Name           | Type  | Owner |   Size    | Description
--------+-------------------------+-------+-------+-----------+-------------
 public | databasechangelog       | table | user  | 16 kB     |
 public | databasechangeloglock   | table | user  | 8192 bytes |
(2 rows)
```

```
test=# \dt my_schema.*
                 List of relations
   Schema   |        Name          | Type  | Owner
------------+----------------------+-------+-------
 my_schema  | airlines             | table | user
 my_schema  | cities               | table | user
 my_schema  | countries            | table | user
 my_schema  | flightavailability   | table | user
 my_schema  | flights              | table | user
 my_schema  | flights_history      | table | user
 my_schema  | maps                 | table | user
 my_schema  | qa_only              | table | user
 my_schema  | schema_only          | table | user
(9 rows)

test=# select count(*) from public.databasechangelog;
 count
-------
    30
(1 row)

test=# select count(*) from my_schema.cities;
 count
-------
    87
(1 row)
```

Back in your shell, we can copy the change set XML generated by post-hook deployment:

```
$ oc rsync $(oc get pods -lapp=dbinit --template='{{range .items}}{{.meta
data.name}}{{end}}'):/data/baseline.xml .
```

You should now have a local copy in your directory of the *baseline.xml* file that contains the database schema change sets generated by the deployment. The file can be stored for reference and later used against other database environments to apply the same schema changes.

Deployment Pod Resources

A deployment is completed by a pod that consumes resources (memory and CPU) on a node. By default, pods consume unbounded node resources. However, if a project specifies default container limits, then pods consume resources up to those limits. Another way to limit resource use is to (optionally) specify resource limits as part of the deployment strategy.

In the busybox welcome app example we looked at earlier, if we wished to limit the CPU to 100 millicores (0.1 CPU units) and memory to 256Mi (256*2^20 bytes), we can specify the resource limit in the deployment config:

```
$ oc patch -n welcome --type=strategic dc myapp \
    -p '{"spec":{"template":{"spec":{"containers":[{"name":"myapp","resources":
{"limits":{"cpu":"100m","memory":"256Mi"}}}]}}}}'
```

When looking at the deployment in the web-ui or from the command line, the limits will be displayed for the pod (Figure 3-2).

CONTAINER: MYAPP

* **Image:** devopswithopenshift/welcome 6778dbf
* **Ports:** 8080/TCP
* **CPU:** 100 millicores limit
* **Memory:** 256 MiB limit

Figure 3-2. Pod resource limits

OpenShift enforces these by using CGroup CPU quota and memory limits in the kernel. More information on deployment pod resources can be found in the product documentation (*http://red.ht/2p2q3Ye*).

We cover project quotas, limits, and container resources in more detail in Chapter 7.

Blue-Green Deployments

The blue-green deployment strategy minimizes the time it takes to perform a deployment cutover by ensuring you have two versions of your application stacks available during the deployment (Figure 3-3). We can make use of the service and routing tiers to easily switch between our two running application stacks—hence it is very simple and fast to perform a rollback.

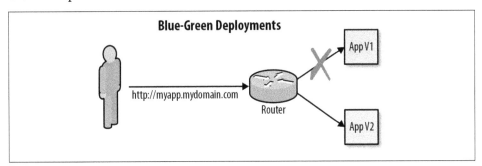

Figure 3-3. Blue-green deployments

Let's deploy both our blue and green applications into the same project and point the bluegreen route to the blue service (Figure 3-4):

```
$ oc new-project bluegreen --display-name="Blue Green Deployments" \
    --description="Blue Green Deployments"
$ oc new-app https://github.com/devops-with-openshift/bluegreen#master \
```

```
    --name=blue
$ oc expose service blue --name=bluegreen
$ oc new-app https://github.com/devops-with-openshift/bluegreen#green \
    --name=green
```

Figure 3-4. Green deployment

We can easily switch the `bluegreen` route to point to either the blue or the green service using the web-ui or the command line:

```
# switch service to green
$ oc patch route/bluegreen -p '{"spec":{"to":{"name":"green"}}}'

# switch back to blue again
$ oc patch route/bluegreen -p '{"spec":{"to":{"name":"blue"}}}'
```

In a stateless application architecture, blue-green deployments can be fairly easy to achieve as you do not have to worry about:

- Long-running transactions in the original blue stack
- Data stores that need to be migrated or rolled back alongside the application

A/B Deployments

A/B deployments get their name from the ability to test the new application features as part of the deployment. This way you can create a hypothesis, perform an A/B deployment, test whether your hypothesis is true or false, and either roll back to your initial application state (A) or proceed with your new application state (B).

A great example is rolling out a change to your sales website or mobile application. You direct a percentage of the traffic to the new version and measure the number of sales by version (conversion rate based on the number of visitors, say). You can then roll back or forward depending on which has the higher conversion rate (Figure 3-5).

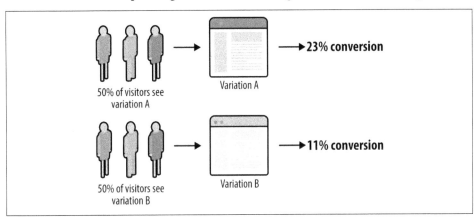

Figure 3-5. A/B testing

We can make use of the OpenShift routing tier to achieve an A/B deployment (Figure 3-6).

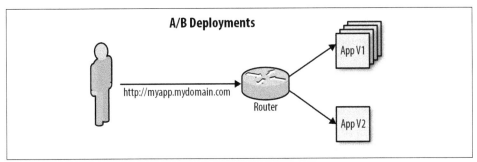

Figure 3-6. A/B deployment

Let's create our application A version using our *Cat of the Day* application:

```
$ oc new-project cotd --display-name='A/B Deployment Example' \
    --description='A/B Deployment Example'
```

```
$ oc new-app --name='cats' -l name='cats' \
    php:5.6~https://github.com/devops-with-openshift/cotd.git \
    -e SELECTOR=cats
$ oc expose service cats --name=cats -l name='cats'
```

Let's create our application *B* version using our *City of the Day* application:

```
$ oc new-app --name='city' -l name='city' \
    php:5.6~https://github.com/devops-with-openshift/cotd.git \
    -e SELECTOR=cities
$ oc expose service city --name=city -l name='city'
```

We also need to override the default *least connection* balance setting of HAProxy using an annotation so that we use *round-robin* and the weightings specified in our `route-backends` command instead:

```
$ oc expose service cats --name='ab' -l name='ab'
$ oc annotate route/ab haproxy.router.openshift.io/balance=roundrobin
$ oc set route-backends ab cats=100 city=0
```

If we browse to the `ab` route we should see Cats. Let's use the OpenShift `set route-backends` command to adjust the weighting through our routing tier so that 10% of the traffic now goes to the City version. We can test hitting the web page 10 times using the `curl` command. The output shows part of the image location in the HTML page, and we can see one 1 out of 10 calls (i.e., 10%) goes to the City version (remember to replace the hostname in the URL with the appropriate name in your environment):

```
$ oc set route-backends ab --adjust city=+10%

$ for i in {1..10}; do curl -s http://ab-cotd.192.168.137.3.xip.io/item.php |
grep "data/.*/images" | awk '{print $5}'; done
 data/cats/images/adelaide.jpg);"
 data/cats/images/adelaide.jpg);"
 data/cats/images/adelaide.jpg);"
 data/cats/images/adelaide.jpg);"
 data/cats/images/adelaide.jpg);"
 data/cats/images/adelaide.jpg);"
 data/cats/images/adelaide.jpg);"
 data/cats/images/adelaide.jpg);"
 data/cities/images/adelaide.jpg);"
 data/cats/images/adelaide.jpg);"
```

The default configuration of the HAProxy is to support sticky sessions using an HAProxy client-side cookie. If you were to mimic a web browser that supports cookies with `curl` (e.g., specify the `--cookie` option), you would only see cats or cities due to the sticky session behavior.

After time, we can measure who likes the most cities or cats based on user feedback logged to both applications. We can use the `oc logs -f <name of pod>` command to see each application's logs:

```
$ oc logs -f $(oc get pods -l name=cats -o name) | grep COTD
...
{"auckland" : "4"}

$ oc logs -f $(oc get pods -l name=city -o name) | grep COTD
...
{"sydney" : "3"}, {"wellington" : "5"}
```

and if we are happy that more users like cities than cats, we can route all our traffic to the B/city version of our application (Figure 3-7):

```
$ oc set route-backends ab cats=0 city=100
```

Which we can see if we look at the Traffic bar in the web-ui:

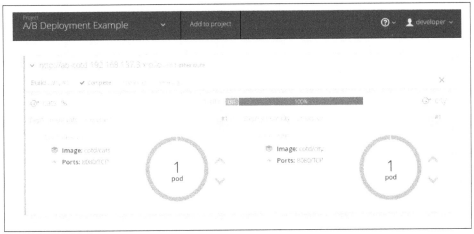

Figure 3-7. All traffic going to (B) cities

Of course in production we are likely to automate the measurement and API calls to set the route weights.

Canary Deployments

A canary deployment is a technique similar to A/B where you slowly roll out the change to a small subset of users before rolling it out to the entire infrastructure and make it available to everybody.

If we look at the A/B example, we can see there are three routes exposed:

```
$ oc get routes
NAME   HOST/PORT                        PATH  SERVICES             PORT
TERMINATION
ab     ab-cotd.192.168.137.3.xip.io           cats(100%),city(0%)  8080-tcp
cats   cats-cotd.192.168.137.3.xip.io         cats                 8080-tcp
city   city-cotd.192.168.137.3.xip.io         city                 8080-tcp
```

We can make use of these to affect a canary deployment strategy:

- One simple strategy is to use a random sample of users for our new version—this is the A/B strategy.

- We could deploy the new version available to internal testers only before releasing to production by directing them to the *City* route for testing.

- Use a *testing project* as a canary—and only promote the change once our tests have passed.

- A more sophisticated approach is to choose users based on their profile and other demographics.

As a cluster admin, you may also take advantage of advanced techniques such as customizing the HAProxy router template configuration (*http://red.ht/2nLzFq5*).

By following the product documentation, you could use custom access control lists (ACLs) to restrict access to our canary route. You do not need to do this now, but here is an example piece of an *haproxy-config.template* that blocks users not in our network subnet from accessing our *city* route:

```
frontend public

    # Custom acl
    # block users not in 192.168.137.0/24 network from accessing city host
    acl network_allowed src 192.168.137.0/24
    acl host_city hdr(host) -i city-cotd.192.168.137.3.xip.io
    acl restricted_page path_beg /
    http-request deny if restricted_page host_city !network_allowed
```

Rollbacks

Rollbacks revert an application back to a previous revision. Blue-green and A/B deployments have inherent rollback capabilities built into them due to both the old and new application versions being available in your environment at the same time.

OpenShift allows you to perform rollbacks on the deployment configuration using the REST API, the CLI, or the web console. Let's use our City/Cats of the Day example to demonstrate a simple rollback of our configuration:

```
$ oc new-project rollback --display-name='Rollback Deployment Example' \
    --description='Rollback Deployment Example'
$ oc new-app --name='cotd' \
    -l name='cotd' php:5.6~https://github.com/devops-with-openshift/cotd.git \
    -e SELECTOR=cats
$ oc expose service cotd --name=cotd -l name='cotd'
```

This will deploy our application with the environment variable SELECTOR set to cats. In the web-ui or from the CLI, we can change the environment variable in our deployment configuration to cities, which will trigger a new deployment displaying cities instead of cats:

```
$ oc env dc cotd SELECTOR=cities
```

Let's see what a rollback to revision 1 of our deployment will look like, but don't perform the rollback:

```
$ oc rollback cotd --to-version=1 --dry-run
...
  Environment Variables:
        SELECTOR:        cats
...
```

We can see the rollback would revert the environment variable SELECTOR back to cats. If no revision is specified with --to-version, then the last successfully deployed revision will be used.

 Image change triggers on the deployment configuration are disabled as part of the rollback to prevent accidentally starting a new deployment process soon after the rollback is complete.

Now perform the rollback, which will trigger a new deployment. There is also a rollback button with settings options available in the web-ui on each numbered deployment to initiate a rollback (Figure 3-8):

```
$ oc rollback cotd --to-version=1
```

Re-enable the image change triggers:

```
$ oc set triggers dc cotd --auto
```

If we now browse to the application URL, we will see cats instead of cities, rolling back our environment variable change. We can also see deployment information in the web-ui or CLI to help us perform rollbacks (or rollforwards!) using:

```
$ oc describe dc cotd
```

If you build a new version of your application, a new deployment will occur as long as the image change trigger is enabled. When rolling back deployment configuration revisions you may also be rolling back the image version depending on what is specified in the deployment configuration.

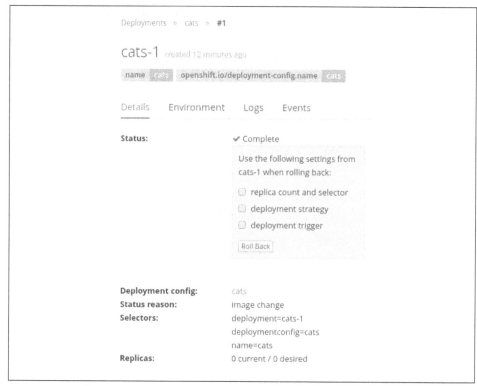

Figure 3-8. Rollback button

Summary

This chapter demonstrated how you can quickly leverage OpenShift's capabilities to automate application deployment. These deployment strategies allow your business services and applications to remain available during deployments of new versions with fast rollback capabilities in case of failure.

By being able to trigger deployments on both image and configuration change, you can automatically and rapidly manage smaller and more frequent updates to applications using OpenShift.

## CHAPTER 4

Pipelines

The Job of the deployment pipeline is to prove that the release candidate is unreleasable.

—Jez Humble

Pipelines allow teams to automate and organize all of the activities required to deliver software changes. By rapidly providing visible feedback, teams can respond and react to failures quickly.

In this chapter we are going to learn about using pipelines inside OpenShift so that we can connect deployment events to the various upstream gates and checks that need to be passed as part of the delivery process.

Our First Pipeline Example

Log in to OpenShift as our user and create a new project. We will follow along using both the web-ui and the command-line interface (choose whichever one you're most comfortable using):

```
$ oc login -u developer -p developer
```

Create a new project called *samplepipeline*:

```
$ oc new-project samplepipeline --display-name="Pipeline Sample" \
    --description='Pipeline Sample'
```

Add the Jenkins ephemeral templated application to the project—it should be an instant app in the catalog which you can check from the web-ui by using Add to Project or from the CLI:

```
$ oc get templates -n openshift | grep jenkins-pipeline-example
jenkins-pipeline-example  This example showcases the new Jenkins Pipeline ...
```

If you have persistent storage and you want to keep your Jenkins build logs after Jenkins Container restarts, then you could use the *jenkins-persistent* template instead.

```
$ oc new-app jenkins-ephemeral
```

In the web-ui continue to the overview page. A Jenkins deployment should be underway, and after the Jenkins images have been pulled from the repository, a pod will be running (Figure 4-1). There are two services created: one for the Jenkins web-ui and the other for the *jenkins-jnlp* service. This is used by the Jenkins slave/agent to interact with the Jenkins application:

```
$ oc get pods
NAME              READY    STATUS    RESTARTS    AGE
jenkins-1-1942b   1/1      Running   0           1m
```

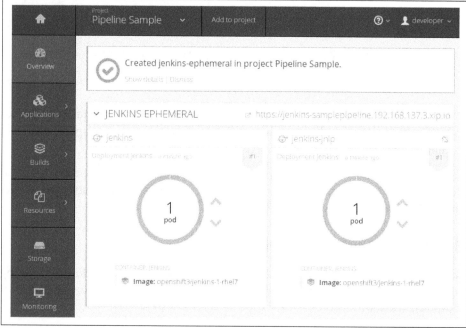

Figure 4-1. The running Jenkins pod with two services

Let's add the example Jenkins pipeline application using the "Add to project" button in Figure 4-1, and the *jenkins-pipeline-example* template:

```
$ oc new-app jenkins-pipeline-example
```

Jenkins Example Application Template

If your installation doesn't have the Jenkins pipeline example template, you can find and load it into OpenShift using this command:

```
$ oc create -f \
https://raw.githubusercontent.com/openshift/origin/
master/examples/jenkins/pipeline/samplepipeline.yaml
```

Once you have hit the Create button, select "Continue to overview". The example application contains a MySQL database; you should see this database pod spin up once the image has been pulled. Let's start the application pipeline build (Figure 4-2). Browse to Builds → Pipelines, and click the Start Pipeline button or use the following command:

```
$ oc start-build sample-pipeline
```

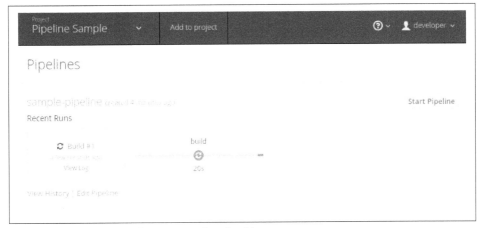

Figure 4-2. Start the application pipeline build

```
$ oc get pods
NAME                                READY   STATUS      RESTARTS   AGE
jenkins-1-ucw9g                     1/1     Running     0          1d    ❶
mongodb-1-t2bxf                     1/1     Running     0          1d    ❷
nodejs-mongodb-example-1-3lhg8      1/1     Running     0          15m   ❸
nodejs-mongodb-example-1-build      0/1     Completed   0          16m   ❹
```

After the build and deploy completes (Figure 4-3), you should be able to see:

❶ The Jenkins server pod.

❷ The MongoDB database pod.

❸ A running Node.js application pod.

❹ And a Completed build pod.

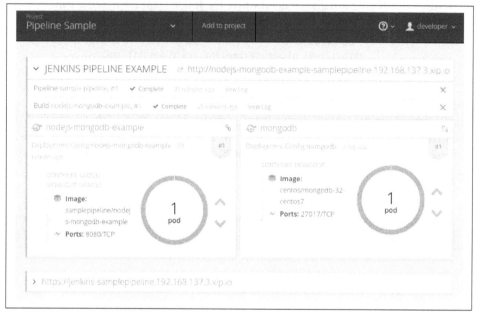

Figure 4-3. Successful pipeline build

If you select the route URL, you should now be able to browse to the running application that increments a page count every time the web page is visited (Figure 4-4).

Figure 4-4. Running pipeline application

Pipeline Components

There are a few moving pieces required to set up a basic flow for continuous testing, integration, and delivery using Jenkins pipelines. Before we look at the details, let's review them at a component level (Figure 4-5).

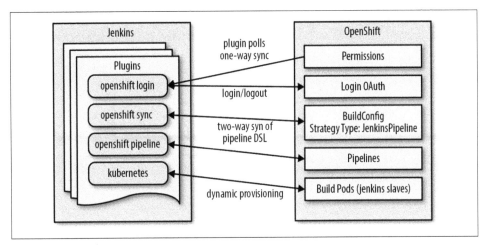

Figure 4-5. Pipeline components

Within Jenkins, the main components and their roles are as follows:

- Jenkins server instance running in a pod on OpenShift
- Jenkins OpenShift Login plug-in: manages login to Jenkins, permissions polling, and one-way synchronization from OpenShift to Jenkins
- Jenkins OpenShift Sync plug-in: two-way synchronization of pipeline build jobs
- Jenkins OpenShift Pipeline plug-in: construction of jobs and workflows for pipelines to work with Kubernetes and OpenShift
- Jenkins Kubernetes plug-in: for provisioning of slave Jenkins builder pods

The product documentation (*http://red.ht/2nceWPX*) is a great place to start for more in-depth reading.

So What's Happened Here? Examination of the Pipeline Details

We've done a lot in a short amount of time! Let's drill down into some of the details to get a better understanding of pipelines in OpenShift. Browse to Builds → Pipelines → sample-pipeline → Configuration in the web-ui, as shown in Figure 4-6.

Figure 4-6. Pipeline configuration

You can see a build strategy of type *Jenkins Pipeline* as well as the *pipeline as code* that is commonly named a *Jenkinsfile*. The pipeline is a Groovy script that tells Jenkins what to do when your pipeline is run.

The commands that are run within each stage make use of the Jenkins OpenShift plug-in (*https://github.com/openshift/jenkins-plugin*). This plug-in provides build and deployment steps via a domain-specific language (DSL) API (in our case, Groovy). So you can see that for a build and deploy we:

- Start the build referenced by the build configuration called *nodejs-mongodb-example*:

```
openshiftBuild(buildConfig: 'nodejs-mongodb-example', showBuildLogs: 'true')
```

- Start the deployment referenced by the deployment configuration called *nodejs-mongodb-example*:

```
openshiftDeploy(deploymentConfig: 'nodejs-mongodb-example')
```

The basic pipeline consists of:

node

> A step that schedules a task to run by adding it to the Jenkins build queue. It may be run on the Jenkins master or slave (in our case, a container). Commands outside of node elements are run on the Jenkins master.

stage

By default, pipeline builds can run concurrently. A stage command lets you mark certain sections of a build as being constrained by limited concurrency.

In the example we have two stages (build and deploy) within a node. When this pipeline is executed by starting a pipeline build, OpenShift runs the build in a build pod, the same as it would with any source to image build. There is also a Jenkins slave pod, which is removed once the build completes successfully. It is this slave pod that communicates back and forth to Jenkins via the *jenkins-jnlp* service.

So, when a build is running, you should be able to see the following pods:

```
$ oc get pods
NAME                            READY   STATUS    RESTARTS   AGE
jenkins-1-ucw9g                 1/1     Running   0          1d    ❶
mongodb-1-t2bxf                 1/1     Running   0          1d    ❷
nodejs-3465c67ce754             1/1     Running   0          51s   ❸
nodejs-mongodb-example-1-build  1/1     Running   0          40s   ❹
```

❶ Jenkins server pod.

❷ MongoDB database pod.

❸ Jenkins slave pod—in this case, a Node.js slave that is removed once the build is completed.

❹ The actual pod running the build of our application.

 Pipeline Basics

To learn more about Jenkins pipeline basics, see the Jenkins pipeline plug-in tutorial for new users (*https://github.com/jenkinsci/pipeline-plugin/blob/master/TUTORIAL.md*).

Explore Jenkins

One of the great features of the integrated pipelines view in OpenShift is that you do not have to drill into Jenkins if you don't want to—all of the pipeline user interface components are available in the OpenShift web-ui. If you want a deeper view of the pipeline in Jenkins, select the *View Log* link on a Pipeline build in your browser.

OAuth Integration

The OpenShift Jenkins image now supports the use of an Open-Shift binding credentials plug-in. This plug-in integrates the Open-Shift OAuth provider with Jenkins so that when users attempt to access Jenkins, they are redirected to authenticate with OpenShift. After authenticating successfully, they are redirected back to the original application with an OAuth token that can be used by the application to make requests on behalf of the user.

Log in to Jenkins with your OpenShift user and password; if OAuth integration is configured, you will have to authorize access as part of the workflow (Figure 4-7).

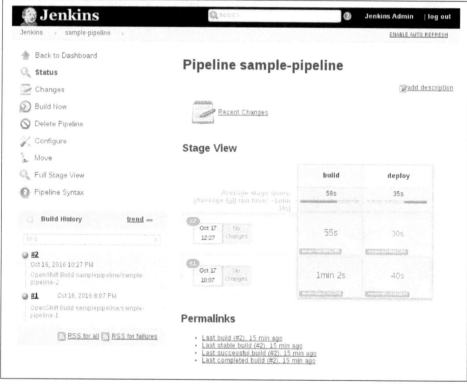

Figure 4-7. Jenkins user interface

There are various editors and drill-down screens within Jenkins available for pipeline jobs. You can browse the build logs and pipeline stage views and configuration. If you are using a newer version of Jenkins, you can also use the Blue Ocean pipeline view (*https://jenkins.io/projects/blueocean*).

Jenkins Slave Images

By default, the Jenkins installation has preconfigured Kubernetes plug-in slave builder images. If you log in to Jenkins and browse to Jenkins → Manage Jenkins → Kubernetes, there are pod templates configured for *Maven* and *Node.js* and you may add in your own custom images. You can convert any OpenShift S2I image into a valid Jenkins slave image using a template; see the full documentation (*http://bit.ly/2tNnNcU*) for extensions.

Multiple Project Pipeline Example

Now that we have the basic pipeline running within a single OpenShift project, the next logical step is to expand our use of pipelines to different projects and namespaces. In a software delivery lifecycle we want to separate out the different pipeline activities such as development, testing, and delivery into production. Within a single OpenShift PaaS cluster we can map these activities to projects. Different collaborating users and groups can access these different projects based on the role-based access control provided by the platform.

Build, Tag, Promote

Ideally we want to build our immutable application images once, then tag the images for promotion into other projects—to perform our pipeline activities such as testing and eventually production deployment. The feedback from our various activities forms the gates for downstream activities. The process of *build*, *tag*, and *promote* forms the foundation for every container-based application to flow through our delivery lifecycle.

We can take the concept further with multiple PaaS instances by using *image registry* integration to promote images between clusters. We may also have an arbitrary number of different activities that can occur that are not specifically linked to environments. Refer to the documentation (*https://blog.openshift.com/cross-cluster-image-promotion-techniques*) for information on cross-cluster promotion techniques.

Common activities such as *user acceptance testing (UAT)* and *pre-production (pre-prod)* can be added into our basic workflow to meet any requirements your organization may have.

So, let's get going on our next pipeline deployment. We are going to set up four projects for our pipeline activities using OpenShift integrated pipelines:

CICD
    Containing our Jenkins instance

Development
> For building and developing our application images

Testing
> For testing our application

Production
> Hosting our production application

Figure 4-8 depicts the general form of our application flow through the various projects (development to testing to production) as well as the access requirements necessary between the projects to allow this flow to occur when using a build, tag, promote strategy. OpenShift authorization policy is managed and configured for project-based service accounts as described in the following section.

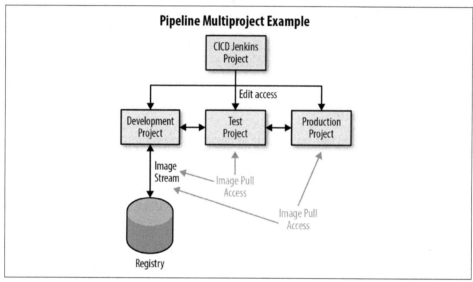

Figure 4-8. Multiple project pipeline

Create Projects

We are going to use the CLI for this more advanced example so we can speed things up a bit. You can, of course, use the web-ui or your IDE if you prefer. Let's create our projects first:

```
$ oc login -u developer -p developer
$ oc new-project cicd --display-name='CICD Jenkins' --description='CICD Jenkins'
$ oc new-project development --display-name='Development' \
    --description='Development'
$ oc new-project testing --display-name='Testing' --description='Testing'
$ oc new-project production --display-name='Production' --description='Produc
tion'
```

Project Name Patterns

It is often useful to create project names and patterns that model an organization. For example:

"organization/tenant"-"environment/activity"-"project"

In this way you can create user groups to a full-tenant, tenant-env, or tenant-env-project and do fine-grained RBAC on it. Also, it's easier to identify from the name to which user the project belongs, in which activity or environment, so you can use the same internal project name on every environment. With this pattern it is easier to avoid project name collisions because within an OpenShift cluster, the project name must be unique.

Add Role-Based Access Control

Let's add in RBAC to our projects to allow the different service accounts to build, promote, and tag images. First we will allow the *cicd* project's Jenkins service account *edit* access to all of our projects:

```
$ oc policy add-role-to-user edit system:serviceaccount:cicd:jenkins \
    -n development
$ oc policy add-role-to-user edit system:serviceaccount:cicd:jenkins \
    -n testing
$ oc policy add-role-to-user edit system:serviceaccount:cicd:jenkins \
    -n production
```

Now we want to allow our testing and production service accounts the ability to pull images from the development project:

```
$ oc policy add-role-to-group system:image-puller system:serviceaccounts:test-
ing \
    -n development
$ oc policy add-role-to-group system:image-puller system:serviceaccounts:produc-
tion \
    -n development
```

Deploy Jenkins and Our Pipeline Definition

Deploy a Jenkins ephemeral instance to our *cicd* project, enable OAuth integration (the default), and set a Java heap size:

```
$ oc project cicd
$ oc new-app --template=jenkins-ephemeral \
    -p JENKINS_IMAGE_STREAM_TAG=jenkins-2-rhel7:latest \
    -p NAMESPACE=openshift \
    -p MEMORY_LIMIT=2048Mi \
    -p ENABLE_OAUTH=true
```

Which Image?

Depending on which version of OpenShift you are using (community OpenShift Origin or the supported OpenShift Container Platform), you may wish to use different base images. The *-1-* series refers to the Jenkins 1.6.X branch, and *-2-* is the Jenkins 2.X branch:

```
jenkins-1-rhel7:latest, jenkins-2-rhel7:latest
    - officially supported Red Hat images from regis-
try.access.redhat.com
jenkins-1-centos7:latest, jenkins-2-centos7:latest
    - community images on hub.docker.io
```

Let's create the pipeline itself using the all-in-one command if you are using the CLI:

```
$ oc create -n cicd -f \
    https://raw.githubusercontent.com/devops-with-openshift/pipeline-configs/
master/pipeline.yaml
```

You could do this manually as well if you wanted to break it down into constituent steps. Add in an empty pipeline definition through the web-ui using Add to project → Import YAML/JSON, and cut and paste an empty pipeline definition:

```
https://raw.githubusercontent.com/devops-with-openshift/pipeline-configs/master/
empty-pipeline.yaml
```

We can then edit the pipeline in the web-ui using Builds → Pipelines → sample-pipeline → Actions → Edit using the following pipeline code, and then pressing Save:

```
https://raw.githubusercontent.com/devops-with-openshift/pipeline-configs/master/
pipeline-groovy.groovy
```

It's worth noting that you can easily create this piece of YAML configuration yourself once you have performed the cut-and-paste exercise. This allows you to rapidly develop and prototype your pipelines as code. Run the following command:

```
$ oc export bc pipeline -o yaml -n cicd
```

Jenkinsfile Path

Rather than embed the pipeline code in the build configuration, it can be extracted into a file and referenced using the jenkinsfile Path parameter. See the OpenShift product documentation (*http://red.ht/2nFeKnM*) for more details.

Deploy Our Sample Application

Let's deploy our sample Cat/City of the Day application into our development project.

 To demonstrate a code change propagating through our environment, you can create a fork of the Git-hosted repository first—so you can check in a source code change that triggers the pipeline webhook automatically.

Invoke *new-app* using the builder image and Git repository URL—remember to replace this with your Git repo. When creating a route, replace the hostname with something appropriate for your environment:

```
$ oc project development
$ oc new-app --name=myapp \
    openshift/php:5.6~https://github.com/devops-with-openshift/cotd.git#master
$ oc expose service myapp --name=myapp \
    --hostname=cotd-development.192.168.137.3.xip.io
```

By default, OpenShift will build and deploy our application in the *development* project and use a *rolling deployment* strategy for any changes. We will be using the *image stream* that has been created to tag and promote into our *testing* and *production* projects, but first we need to create *deployment configuration* items in those projects.

To create the deployment configuration, you first need to know the IP address of the *Docker registry* service for your deployment. By default, the *development* user does not have permission to read from the *default* namespace, so we can also glean this information from the development image stream:

```
$ oc get is -n development
NAME      DOCKER REPO                            TAGS      UPDATED
myapp     172.30.18.201:5000/development/myapp   latest    13 minutes ago
```

As a cluster admin user, you may also look at the Docker registry service directly:

```
$ oc get svc docker-registry -n default
NAME              CLUSTER-IP      EXTERNAL-IP    PORT(S)    AGE
docker-registry   172.30.18.201   <none>         5000/TCP   18d   ❶
```

❶ Cluster IP address and port for the docker registry. See the product *services* documentation (*http://red.ht/2oExVTo*) for more information.

Create the deployment configuration in the *testing* project. Be sure to use your own environment registry IP address. Every time we change or edit the deployment configuration, a configuration trigger causes a deployment to occur. We cancel the automatically triggered deployment because we haven't used our pipeline to build, tag,

and promote our image yet—so the deployment would run until it timed out waiting
for the correctly tagged image:

```
$ oc project testing
$ oc create dc myapp --image=172.30.18.201:5000/development/myapp:promoteQA
$ oc deploy myapp --cancel
```

One change we need to make in *testing* is to update the `imagePullPolicy` for our
container. By default, it is set to `IfNotPresent`, but we wish to *always* trigger a
deployment when we tag a new image:

```
$ oc patch dc/myapp \
    -p '{"spec":{"template":{"spec":{"containers":[{"name":"default-
container","imagePullPolicy":"Always"}]}}}}'
$ oc deploy myapp --cancel
```

Let's also create our service and route while we're at it (be sure to change the hostname to suit your environment):

```
$ oc expose dc myapp --port=8080
$ oc expose service myapp --name=myapp \
    --hostname=cotd-testing.192.168.137.3.xip.io
```

Repeat these steps for the production project:

```
$ oc project production
$ oc create dc myapp --image=172.30.18.201:5000/development/myapp:promotePRD
$ oc deploy myapp --cancel
$ oc patch dc/myapp \
    -p '{"spec":{"template":{"spec":{"containers":[{"name":"default-
container","imagePullPolicy":"Always"}]}}}}'
$ oc deploy myapp --cancel
$ oc expose dc myapp --port=8080
$ oc expose service myapp --hostname=cotd-production.192.168.137.3.xip.io --
name=myapp
```

We are using two separate (arbitrary) image tags: *promoteQA* for testing promotion
and *promotePRD* for production promotion.

Run Our Pipeline Deployment

Now we are ready to run our pipeline deployment from the *cicd* project:

```
$ oc start-build pipeline -n cicd
```

You should be able to see the pipeline build progressing using the web-ui in the *cicd*
project by navigating to Browse → Builds → Pipeline (Figure 4-9).

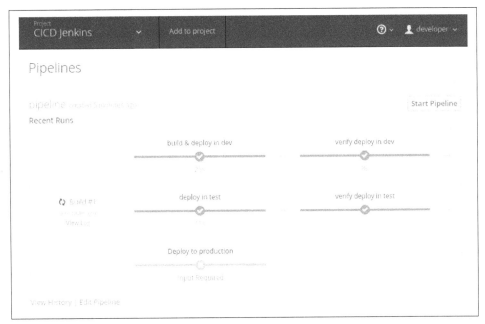

Figure 4-9. Complex pipeline running

If we browse to the *testing* project, we can also see two pods spun up and deployed. We could then run automated or manual test steps against this environment. A testing environment on-demand—great!

We can also see that the pipeline is paused waiting for user input. If you select Input Required you will be taken to the running Jenkins (you may have to log in if you haven't already). Select Proceed to allow the pipeline to continue to deploy to production (Figure 4-10).

Figure 4-10. Manually approve deployment to production

If you browse back to the *production* project, you'll now see that two pods deployed OK, and if you browse to the production application URL, you should be able to see our City of the Day.

Hold on a second! That's a cat. It looks like we deployed the wrong branch of code into our environments—perhaps our testing wasn't as great as we thought.

Quickly Deploying a New Branch

Go to the *development* project and browse to Builds → Builds → myapp → Actions → Edit. We can change the branch by changing *master* in the *Source Repository Ref* to *feature*.

```
$ oc project development
$ oc patch bc/myapp -p '{"spec":{"source":{"git":{"ref":"feature"}}}}'
```

Let's start another pipeline build, but this time do some manual testing to ensure we get the right results before we deploy to production:

```
$ oc start-build pipeline -n cicd
```

That looks better. Manually approve the changes into our *production* environment (Figure 4-11).

Figure 4-11. City of the Day (take 2)

Managing Image Changes

Operations teams looking to adopt containers in production have to think about software supply chains and how they can help developers to sensibly adopt and choose supported enterprise-grade containers on which to base their own software. Given that a container image is made up of layers, it is very important that developers and operations teams are aware of what's going into their containers as early in the development lifecycle as possible.

Containers converge the software supply chain that makes up the layered build artifact (Figure 4-12). Infra/ops still needs to update the underlying standard operating environment, while developers can cleanly separate their own code and deliver it free of impediments. Both teams can operate at a speed or cadence that suits, only changing their pieces of the container repository when they need to. Incompatibilities can be surfaced early during build instead of at deploy time, and tests can be used to increase confidence.

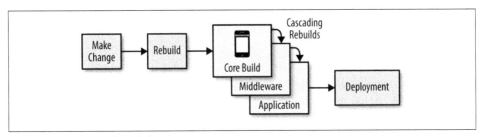

Figure 4-12. Image build chain

The core build will contain enough of the operating system to run the middleware and application. If you are using one of the Red Hat base builder images, that will already provide middleware for your application. In our City of the Day application we can easily see build chain dependencies using the `oc adm build-chain` command:

```
$ oc login -u sysadmin:admin
$ oc adm build-chain php:5.6 -n openshift --all
<openshift istag/php:5.6>
  <development bc/myapp>
    <development istag/myapp:latest>
```

The `build-chain` command is great because it can create pictures of the dependencies. I have created a new playground namespace using the same image and application deployed—let's have a look at the build chain dependecies (Figure 4-13):

```
$ oc adm build-chain php:5.6 -n openshift --all -o dot   | dot -T svg -o deps.svg
```

dot Utility

To run this command you may need to install the *dot* utility from the *graphviz* package. For RPM-based Linux systems:

```
$ yum install graphviz
```

See *http://www.graphviz.org/Download.php* for other systems (Mac, Windows, other Linux distros).

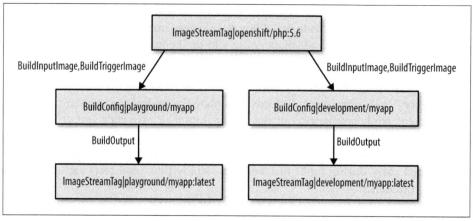

Figure 4-13. ImageStream dependencies

We can easily determine if a change in our base builder image php:5.6 will cause a change in our application stack. This deployment uses an *Image Change Trigger* (*http://red.ht/2oDl1Fx*) on the build configuration to detect that a new image is available in OpenShift. When the image changes, our dependent applications are built and redeployed automatically in our development and playground projects.

We can see the trigger in the build configuration (YAML/JSON) or by inspecting:

```
$ oc project development
$ oc set triggers bc/myapp --all
NAME                 TYPE     VALUE                AUTO
buildconfigs/myapp   config                        true
buildconfigs/myapp   image    openshift/php:5.6    true    ❶
buildconfigs/myapp   webhook  gqBsJ6bdHVdjiEfZi8Up
buildconfigs/myapp   github   uAmMxR1uQnW66plqmKOt
```

❶ Build configuration image change trigger

But what if we want the pipeline to manage our build and deployment based on a base image change?

Cascading Pipelines

Lets take a simple layered Dockerfile build strategy example. We have two Dockerfiles that we are going to use to layer up our image in this example. The layers are related to each other using the standard *FROM* image definition in the Dockerfile. For example:

```
Layered Image
 _____
| app layer (foo app)     |  ❸
| ----------------------- |
| ops layer (middleware)  |  ❷
| ----------------------- |
| busybox                 |  ❶
|_____|
```

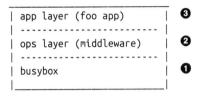

❶   Base busybox image from Dockerhub

❷   ops middleware layer—a shell script

❸   foo application layer built from ops image

Now, we have arbitrarily made this example pretty simple and our operations managed middleware layer is a simple shell script! We are going to run through a worked example, but this is how you would write the Dockerfiles:

```
# middleware ops/Dockerfile
FROM docker.io/busybox
ADD ./hello.sh ./
EXPOSE 8080
CMD ["./hello.sh"]

# application foo/Dockerfile
FROM welcome/ops:latest
CMD ["./hello.sh","foo"]
```

Now, what we would like is a pipeline build of the *foo* application being triggered when the ops application image is rebuilt (either manually, or because a new *busybox* image is pushed into our registry).

Let's set up our welcome project and give the Jenkins service account edit access:

```
$ oc login -u developer -p developer
$ oc new-project welcome --display-name='Welcome' --description='Welcome'
$ oc policy add-role-to-user edit system:serviceaccount:cicd:jenkins -n welcome
```

Next we create builds for the *ops* and *foo* applications. We need to wait for the ops:latest image to exist before we can create and build foo, or we could use the --allow-missing-imagestream-tags flag on the foo new-app command:

```
$ oc new-build --context-dir=sh --name=ops --strategy=docker \
    https://github.com/devops-with-openshift/welcome
$ oc new-build --context-dir=foo --name=foo --strategy=docker \
    --allow-missing-imagestream-tags \
    https://github.com/devops-with-openshift/welcome
```

Once the foo build completes, deploy our newly built image, and create a service and a route for the *foo* application:

```
$ oc create dc foo --image=172.30.18.201:5000/welcome/foo:latest
$ oc expose dc foo --port=8080
$ oc expose svc foo
```

We can test the running *foo* application:

```
$ curl foo-welcome.192.168.137.3.xip.io
Hello foo ! Welcome to OpenShift 3
```

Let's create our *welcome* and *foo* pipeline builds in the *cicd* project we created earlier:

```
$ oc create -n cicd -f \
    https://raw.githubusercontent.com/devops-with-openshift/pipeline-configs/
master/ops-pipeline.yaml
```

We can then set up the build configuration triggers. We want to disable the build configuration `ImageChange` trigger from our *foo* application—because we want our *foo* pipeline build to manage this build and deployment:

```
$ oc set triggers bc foo --from-image='ops:latest' --remove -n welcome
```

We now want to add the `ImageChange` trigger to our *foo* pipeline build configuration —so that every time a new *welcome* image is pushed, our pipeline build will start:

```
$ oc patch bc foo -n cicd \
    -p '{"spec":{"triggers":[{"type":"ImageChange","imageChange":{"from":
{"kind":"ImageStreamTag","namespace": "welcome","name": "ops:latest"}}}]}}'
```

Similarly, we want to remove the build configuration `ImageChange` trigger from our *welcome* application—because we want our *welcome* pipeline build to manage this build and deployment when the *busybox:latest* image changes:

```
$ oc set triggers bc ops --from-image='busybox:latest' --remove -n welcome
$ oc patch bc ops -n cicd \
    -p '{"spec":{"triggers":[{"type":"ImageChange","imageChange":{"from":
{"kind":"ImageStreamTag","namespace": "welcome","name": "busybox:latest"}}}]}}'
```

Let's test things out by triggering a *welcome* pipeline application build and deployment. What we expect to see is a new *foo* pipeline build start automatically once the *welcome:latest* image is pushed:

```
$ oc start-build ops -n cicd
```

We now have cascading build and deployment pipelines that we can use to manage our various image changes (Figure 4-14). These pipelines can be managed separately by different teams with different cadences for change. For example, the *ops* pipeline may be run and changed occasionally for security patching or updates. The *foo* application will be changed and run regularly by developers.

The pipelines can also be arbitrarily complex—for example, we would want to include testing of our images! We may also wish to manage the pipelines across separate projects and namespaces. So we have a basic *InfraOps pipeline* along with a *Developer pipeline*.

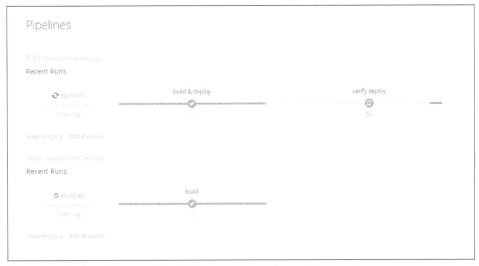

Figure 4-14. Cascading pipeline deployment using ImageChange triggers

Customizing Jenkins

There are several important things you will need to consider when running Jenkins as part of integrated pipelines on OpenShift. The product documentation (*http://red.ht/2oEhcPQ*) is a great place to learn about these. We are going to cover some important choices here.

The Jenkins template deployed as part of integrated pipeline is configured in the OpenShift master configuration file. By default, this is usually the ephemeral (non-persistent) Jenkins template. You can change this behavior by editing the `template Name` and `templateNamespace` field of the `jenkinsPipelineConfig` stanza. To keep all of your historical build jobs after a Jenkins container restart, you can provision the `jenkins-persistent` template and provide a `PersistentVolume` to keep those records in.

You may also wish to turn on auto-provisioning of a Jenkins instance when a pipeline build configuration is deployed by setting the `autoProvisionEnabled: true` flag. You can set template parameters in the `parameters` section of the master config `jenkinsPipelineConfig` section (*openshift.local.config/master/master-config.yaml*):

```
jenkinsPipelineConfig:
  autoProvisionEnabled: true
  parameters:
    JENKINS_IMAGE_STREAM_TAG: jenkins-2-rhel7:latest
    ENABLE_OAUTH: "true"
  serviceName: jenkins
  templateName: jenkins-ephemeral
  templateNamespace: openshift
```

With these settings, when you deploy the sample pipeline application example:

```
$ oc new-app jenkins-pipeline-example
```

an ephemeral Jenkins instance using the supported *jenkins-2-rhel7:latest* image is automatically created with OAuth enabled. To customize the official OpenShift Container Platform Jenkins image, you have two options:

- Use Docker layering
- Use the Jenkins image as a source to image builder

If you are using persistent storage for Jenkins, you could also add plug-ins through the Manage Jenkins → Manage Plugins admin page that will persist across restarts. This is not considered very maintainable because the configuration is manually applied. You may also wish to extend the base Jenkins image by adding your own plug-ins—for example, by adding in:

SonarQube (http://bit.ly/SonarQube)
    For continuous inspection of code quality.

OWASP (http://bit.ly/OWASPDepCheck)
    Dependency check plug-in that detects known vulnerabilities in project dependencies.

Ansible (http://bit.ly/AnsiblePlug)
    Plug-in that allows you to add Ansible tasks as a job build step.

Multibranch (http://bit.ly/MultibranchPlug)
    Plug-in to handle code branching in a single group.

This way, your customized, reusable Jenkins image will contain all the tooling you need to support more complex CICD pipeline jobs—you can perform code quality checks, check for vulnerabilities (continuous security) in your dependencies at build and deployment time, as well as run Ansible playbooks to help provision off-PaaS resources.

The multibranch plug-in will automatically create a new Jenkins job whenever a new branch is pushed to a source code repository. Other plug-ins can define various branch types (e.g., a Git branch, a Subversion branch, a GitHub pull request, etc.). This is extremely useful when we want to reuse our `Jenkinsfile` pipeline as code definitions across branches, especially if we are doing bug-fixing or feature enhancements on branches and merging back to trunk when completed.

See the product documentation (*http://red.ht/2nceWPX*) for more details on customizing the Jenkins image.

Extending Your Pipelines Using Libraries

There are some great dynamic and reusable Jenkins pipeline libraries that you can use within your own pipelines as code that offer a lot of reusable features:

Fabric8 Pipeline for Jenkins (http://bit.ly/Fabric8GH)
    Provides a set of reusable Jenkins pipeline steps and functions.

Jenkinsfiles Library (http://bit.ly/JenkinsfileGH)
    Provides a set of reusable Jenkinsfile files you can use on your projects.

Parallel Build Jobs

An important part of running jobs *fast* within our pipeline is the ability to run each node in parallel if we choose. We can use the Groovy keyword *parallel* to achieve this. Running lots of tests in parallel is a good example use case:

```
stage 'parallel'
parallel 'unitTests': {
        node('maven') {
            echo 'This stage runs automated unit tests'
            // code ...
        }
    }, 'sonarAnalysis': {
        node('maven') {
            echo 'This stage runs the code quality tests'
            // code ...
        }
    }, 'seleniumTests': {
        node('maven') {
            echo 'This stage runs the web user interface tests'
            // code ...
        }
    }, failFast: true
```

When we execute this pipeline, we can look at the pods created to run this job, or inspect the Jenkins logs:

```
[unitTests]     Running on maven-38d93137cc2 in /tmp/workspace/parallel
[sonarAnalysis] Running on maven-38fc49f8a37 in /tmp/workspace/parallel
[seleniumTests] Running on maven-392189bf779 in /tmp/workspace/parallel
```

We can see three different slave builder pods were launched to run each node. This makes it easy to run steps at the same time, making our pipelines faster to execute as well as making use of the elasticity OpenShift provides for running build steps in containers on demand.

Summary

This chapter demonstrated how you can readily use integrated pipelines with your OpenShift projects. Automating each gate and step in a pipeline allows you to visibly feed back the results of your activities to teams, allowing you to react fast when failures occur. The ability to continually iterate what you put in your pipeline is a great way to deliver quality software fast. Use pipeline capabilities to easily create container applications on demand for all of your build, test, and deployment requirements.

## CHAPTER 5

Configuration Management

In software engineering it is recommended to separate dynamic configuration from static runtime software. This allows developers and operations engineers to change the configuration without having to rebuild the runtime.

In OpenShift it is recommended to only have runtime software packaged into a container image and stored in the registry. Configuration is then injected into the image at runtime during the initialization stage. A substantial benefit of this approach is that the runtime image can be built once while the configuration can change as the application is promoted between different environments (e.g., dev to test to production).

OpenShift has a number of mechanisms by which configuration can be added to a running pod:

- Secrets
- Configuration maps
- Environment variables
- Downward API
- Layered builds

In the following sections we will go through the pros and cons of each mechanism.

Secrets

As the name suggests, secrets are a mechanism by which sensitive information (e.g., usernames/passwords/certificates) can be added to pods.

Secret Creation

To create a secret, use the `oc secret` command:

```
$ oc secret new test-secret cert.pem

secret/test-secret
```

With multiple files contained in the secret:

```
$ oc secret new ssl-secret keys=key.pem certs=cert.pem

secret/ssl-secret
```

 When creating secrets with multiple fields, the keys used to identify the individual files need to correspond to the following convention rfc1035/rfc1123 subdomain (DNS_SUBDOMAIN):

```
$ oc get secrets
NAME             TYPE        DATA       AGE
ssl-secret       Opaque      2          48s
test-secret      Opaque      1          8m
```

For more information, see *https://github.com/kubernetes/kuber netes/blob/master/docs/design/identifiers.md*.

For management purposes, secrets can also have labels assigned to them with the `oc label` command:

```
$ oc label secret ssl-secret env=test

secret "ssl-secret" labeled

$ oc get secrets --show-labels=true
```

```
NAME             TYPE        DATA      AGE       LABELS
ssl-secret       Opaque      2         25s       env=test
```

Removing secrets is as simple as using the `oc delete secret` command:

```
$ oc delete secret ssl-secret

secret "ssl-secret" deleted
```

Using Secrets in Pods

Once the secret is created it needs to be added to the pod. There are two methods by which to do this:

- Mounting the secret as a volume

- Injecting the secret as an environment variable

In the following example we are going to use OCP resources created by executing the following command:

```
$ oc new-app https://github.com/openshift/nodejs-ex
```

Mounting as a volume

The secret is added as a volume to the underlying deployment config. For example:

```
$ oc get dc| grep nodejs-ex

NAME          REVISION   DESIRED   CURRENT   TRIGGERED BY
node-canary   2          1         1         config,image(nodejs-ex:canary)
nodejs-ex     16         1         1         config,image(nodejs-ex:latest)


$ oc volume dc/nodejs-ex --add -t secret --secret-name=ssl-secret -m /etc/keys \
  --name=ssl-keys deploymentconfigs/nodejs-ex
```

Adding the volume will result in the firing of the config change trigger and the pods will be redeployed.

To verify that the secrets are mounted under Volume Mounts, run the following command:

```
$ oc describe pod nodejs-ex-21-apdcg

Name:               nodejs-ex-21-apdcg
Namespace:          node-dev
Security Policy:    restricted
Node:               192.168.65.2/192.168.65.2
Start Time:         Sat, 22 Oct 2016 15:48:26 +1100
Labels:             app=nodejs-ex
            deployment=nodejs-ex-21
            deploymentconfig=nodejs-ex
Status:             Running
IP:                 172.17.0.13
Controllers:        ReplicationController/nodejs-ex-21
Containers:
  nodejs-ex:
    Container ID:   docker://
255be1c595fc2654468ab0f0df2f99715ac3f05d1773d05c59a18534051f2933
    Image:          172.30.18.34:5000/node-dev/nodejs-
ex@sha256:891f5118149f1f134330d1ca6fc9756ded5dcc6f810e251473e3eeb02095ea95
    Image ID:       docker://
sha256:6a0eb3a95c6c2387bea75dbe86463e31ab1e1ed7ee1969b446be6f0976737b8c
    Port:           8080/TCP
    State:          Running
      Started:      Sat, 22 Oct 2016 15:48:27 +1100
    Ready:          True
    Restart Count:  0
```

```
    Volume Mounts:
      /etc/keys from ssl-keys (rw)
      /var/run/secrets/kubernetes.io/serviceaccount from default-token-lr5yp
  (ro)
    Environment Variables:    <none>
```

Alternatively:

```
$ oc get pod nodejs-ex-21-apdcg -o \
    jsonpath="{.spec.containers[*]['volumeMounts']}"

[{ssl-keys false /etc/keys } {default-token-lr5yp true /var/run/secrets/kuber-
netes.io/serviceaccount }]
```

The files contained within the secret will be available in the */var/keys* directory.

```
$ oc rsh nodejs-ex-22-8noey ls  /etc/keys

certs  keys
```

Mounting secrets as environment variables

It is also possible to mount the contents of secrets as environment variables.

First, create the secret:

```
$ oc secret new env-secrets username=user-file password=password-file

secret/env-secrets
```

Then add it to the deployment config:

```
$ oc set env dc/nodejs-ex --from=secret/env-secrets

deploymentconfig "nodejs-ex" updated

$ oc describe pod nodejs-ex-22-8noey

Name:            nodejs-ex-22-8noey
Namespace:         node-dev
Security Policy:    restricted
Node:            192.168.65.2/192.168.65.2
Start Time:        Sat, 22 Oct 2016 16:37:35 +1100
Labels:            app=nodejs-ex
          deployment=nodejs-ex-22
          deploymentconfig=nodejs-ex
Status:          Running
IP:            172.17.0.14
Controllers:        ReplicationController/nodejs-ex-22
Containers:
  nodejs-ex:
    Container ID:    docker://
a129d112ca8ee730b7d8a41a51439e1189c7557fa917a852c50e539903e2721a
    Image:        172.30.18.34:5000/node-dev/nodejs-
ex@sha256:891f5118149f1f134330d1ca6fc9756ded5dcc6f810e251473e3eeb02095ea95
```

```
    Image ID:          docker://
sha256:6a0eb3a95c6c2387bea75dbe86463e31ab1e1ed7ee1969b446be6f0976737b8c
    Port:          8080/TCP
    State:          Running
      Started:          Sat, 22 Oct 2016 16:37:36 +1100
    Ready:          True
    Restart Count:    0
    Volume Mounts:
      /var/keys from ssl-keys (rw)
      /var/run/secrets/kubernetes.io/serviceaccount from default-token-lr5yp
(ro)
    Environment Variables:

      PASSWORD:      <set to the key 'password' in secret 'env-secrets'>
      USERNAME:      <set to the key 'username' in secret 'env-secrets'>

$ oc env dc/nodejs-ex --list

# deploymentconfigs nodejs-ex, container nodejs-ex
# PASSWORD from secret env-secrets, key password
# USERNAME from secret env-secrets, key username
```

 Something to be aware of with secrets is that if the user gets access to the pod (e.g., by using the oc rsh command), the user will be able to see the contents of the secrets either in the environment variables or in the volume mounts. While the secrets mechanism ensures that the data in the secret is never stored at rest on the node, it is the user's responsibility to ensure the secrecy of the contents.

It is recommended that the contents of the secret be encrypted or obfuscated before creation. Secrets are stored internally in the *etcd* datastore as Base64-encoded strings which may not be secure enough in certain environments.

Additional Information

Secrets are intended to store only small amounts of data, and each secret is limited to a maximum size of 1 MB. From an administrator's perspective the number of secrets a user can create is controllable via OpenShift ResourceQuotas.

Secrets are not shared across namespaces/projects; they need to be created in each environment in which they're required. Secrets also need to be created before the pods that use them. If the secret isn't there the dependent pods will fail to start.

Injected secrets are also idempotent from the perspective that any external changes such as modification or removal will not be reflected in the dependent pods. To receive any updates to the secrets, the dependent pods need to be restarted.

Secrets are primarily intended to be used for binary configuration items such as SSL keys and certificates as well as username and password. For larger string-based configuration, configuration maps may be a better fit.

Configuration Maps

Configuration maps are very similar to secrets but are intended to contain nonsensitive text-based configuration. Similar to secrets, they can be injected into pods either by being mounted as a volume into the filesystem or set as environment variables.

A major difference between configuration maps and secrets is how they handle updates. When the content of a configuration map is changed, this is reflected in the pod's that it's mounted in and the contents of the files in the pod's filesystem are changed. Configuration maps mounted as environment variables do not change.

To maximize the benefit of this feature, applications should be written to take advantage of dynamically changing configuration files. There are a number of libraries that can help with this, including Apache Commons Configuration or Spring Cloud Kubernetes for Java.

It is common to have pods using both secrets and configuration maps simultaneously to configure the running container. See Figure 5-1.

Creating Configuration Maps

Configuration maps can be created containing one or more text files as well as literal string values:

```
$ oc create configmap test-config --from-literal=key1=config1 \
  --from-literal=key2=config2 --from-file=filters.properties

configmap "test-config" created
```

Mounting Configuration Maps as Volumes

We can also mount configuration maps as volumes that are readable within our container:

```
$ oc volume dc/nodejs-ex --add -t configmap  -m /etc/config --name=app-config \
  --configmap-name=test-config

deploymentconfigs/nodejs-ex
```

The configuration map will be available as files in the */etc/config* directory:

```
$ oc rsh nodejs-ex-26-44kdm ls /etc/config

filters.properties  key1  key2
```

To dynamically change the configuration map, delete it and recreate. The pods using it will be updated automatically without the pod restarting:

```
$ oc delete configmap test-config
configmap "test-config" deleted

$ oc create configmap test-config --from-literal=key1=config3 \
    --from-literal=key2=config4 --from-literal=key3=test \
    --from-file=filters.properties

configmap "test-config" created

$ oc rsh nodejs-ex-26-44kdm ls /etc/config

filters.properties  key1  key2 key3
```

Figure 5-1. Secrets and configuration maps in the same pod

Mounting the Configuration Map as Environment Variables

It is also possible to mount configuration map entries as environment variables (Figure 5-2):

```
$ oc set env dc/nodejs-ex --from=configmap/test-config

deploymentconfig "nodejs-ex" updated

$ oc describe pod nodejs-ex-27-mqurr
```

```
Name:              nodejs-ex-27-mqurr
Namespace:         node-dev
Security Policy:   restricted
Node:              192.168.65.2/192.168.65.2
Start Time:        Sat, 22 Oct 2016 21:15:57 +1100
Labels:            app=nodejs-ex
                 deployment=nodejs-ex-27
                 deploymentconfig=nodejs-ex
Status:            Running
IP:                172.17.0.13
Controllers:         ReplicationController/nodejs-ex-27
Containers:
  nodejs-ex:
    Container ID:    docker://
b095481dfae40855815afe46dc61086957a99c907edb5a26fed1a39ed559e725
    Image:           172.30.18.34:5000/node-dev/nodejs-
ex@sha256:891f5118149f1f134330d1ca6fc9756ded5dcc6f810e251473e3eeb02095ea95
    Image ID:        docker://
sha256:6a0eb3a95c6c2387bea75dbe86463e31ab1e1ed7ee1969b446be6f0976737b8c
    Port:            8080/TCP
    State:           Running
      Started:         Sat, 22 Oct 2016 21:15:59 +1100
    Ready:           True
    Restart Count:   0
    Volume Mounts:
      /etc/config from app-config (rw)
      /var/run/secrets/kubernetes.io/serviceaccount from default-token-lr5yp
(ro)
    Environment Variables:
      FILTERS_PROPERTIES:    <set to the key 'filters.properties' of config map
'test-config'>
      KEY1:                  <set to the key 'key1' of config map 'test-config'>
      KEY2:                  <set to the key 'key2' of config map 'test-config'>
```

Figure 5-2. Environment variables

Environment Variables

As seen previously, both elements of secrets and configuration maps can be added to pods as environment variables. It is also possible to explicitly add and remove environment variables on their own.

 Adding, removing, and modifying environment variables will result in the ConfigChange trigger firing (if configured). See "Change Triggers" on page 70.

Adding Environment Variables

The following command adds a number of individual environment variables to a deployment configuration and hence will be added to all pods running under its control:

```
$ oc set env dc/nodejs-ex ENV=TEST_ENV DB_ENV=TEST1 AUTO_COMMIT=true

deploymentconfig "nodejs-ex" updated


$ oc set env dc/nodejs-ex --list

# deploymentconfigs nodejs-ex, container nodejs-ex
AUTO_COMMIT=true
DB_ENV=TEST1
ENV=TEST_ENV
```

Removing Environment Variables

Removing environment variables is just as straightforward as the following command demonstrates. Once again the pods under the control of the deployment configuration will be restarted, assuming configuration change triggers are enabled (we'll discuss this further in the section that follows):

```
$ oc set env dc/nodejs-ex DB_ENV-

deploymentconfig "nodejs-ex" updated

$ oc env dc/nodejs-ex --list

# deploymentconfigs nodejs-ex, container nodejs-ex
AUTO_COMMIT=true
ENV=TEST_ENV
```

It's possible to both add and remove environment variables at the same time:

```
$ oc env dc/nodejs-ex ENV=TEST_ENV  AUTO_COMMIT- MOCK=FALSE

deploymentconfig "nodejs-ex" updated

$ oc env dc/nodejs-ex --list

# deploymentconfigs nodejs-ex, container nodejs-ex
ENV=TEST_ENV
MOCK=FALSE
```

Change Triggers

OpenShift currently supports two change triggers within the deployment configuration. If either of these triggers are fired, the deployment configuration will restart the pods under its control.

ImageChange *trigger*
> Fires when the underlying image stream changes (e.g., new build or import).

ConfigChange *trigger*
> Fires when the configuration of the pod template within the DeploymentConfig is changed.

It's possible to disable one or both triggers. If a number of configuration changes are required—say, adding both configuration maps and secrets—it may be preferable to disable the ConfigChange trigger, add the required resources, and then re-enable the trigger again.

In the following example, take notice of the pod name. With ConfigChangeTriggers disabled the pod is not restarted until explicitly done so via the oc deploy command, whereas the pod would automatically be restarted after each change if ConfigChange Triggers is enabled:

```
$ oc set triggers dc/nodejs-ex --from-config --remove

deploymentconfig "nodejs-ex" updated

$ oc get pods

NAME                   READY    STATUS    RESTARTS   AGE
nodejs-ex-35-iyefb     1/1      Running   0          9m

$ oc volume dc/nodejs-ex --add -t secret --secret-name=ssl-secret -m /etc/keys
--name=ssl-keys

deploymentconfigs/nodejs-ex

$ oc volume dc/nodejs-ex --add -t configmap  -m /etc/config --name=app-config \
```

```
    --configmap-name=test-config

deploymentconfigs/nodejs-ex

$ oc env dc/nodejs-ex ENV=TEST_ENV DB_ENV=TEST1 AUTO_COMMIT=true

deploymentconfig "nodejs-ex" updated

$ oc get pods

NAME                  READY    STATUS     RESTARTS   AGE
nodejs-ex-35-iyefb    1/1      Running    0          9m

$ oc set triggers dc/nodejs-ex --from-config

deploymentconfig "nodejs-ex" updated

$ oc get pods

NAME                  READY    STATUS     RESTARTS   AGE
nodejs-ex-35-iyefb    1/1      Running    0          9m  <-- Not restarted

$ oc deploy dc/nodejs-ex --latest

Started deployment #36
Use 'oc logs -f dc/nodejs-ex' to track its progress.

$ oc get pods

NAME                  READY    STATUS     RESTARTS   AGE
nodejs-ex-36-px3nq    1/1      Running    0          4s   <-- Pod restarted

$ oc env dc/nodejs-ex --list

# deploymentconfigs nodejs-ex, container nodejs-ex
ENV=TEST_ENV
DB_ENV=TEST1
AUTO_COMMIT=true

$ oc volumes dc/nodejs-ex

deploymentconfigs/nodejs-ex
  secret/ssl-secret as ssl-keys
    mounted at /etc/keys
  unknown as app-config
    mounted at /etc/config
```

Labels and Annotations

One of the most powerful features of OpenShift/Kubernetes is the platform's support for metadata. Two primary mechanisms can be used to configure and access metadata:

- Labels
- Annotations

Labels are identifying metadata consisting of key/value pairs attached to resources. Labels are used to add identifying attributes to objects that are relevant to users and can be used to reflect architectural or organizational concepts. Labels can be used in conjunction with label selectors to uniquely identify individual resources or groups of resources.

Label examples

- Release
- Environment
- Relationship
- DMZBased
- Tier
- Node types
- User type

Annotations are similar to labels but primarily concerned with attaching non-identifying information, which is primarily used by other clients such as tools or libraries. Annotations don't have the concept of selectors.

Annotation examples

- *example.com/skipValidation=true*
- *example.com/MD5Checksum=23798FGH*
- *example.com/BUILDDATE=3479845*

Downward API

The Downward API is a mechanism whereby pods can retrieve their metadata without having to call into the Kubernetes API. The following metadata can be retrieved and used to configure the running pods:

- Labels
- Annotations
- Pod name, namespace, and IP address
- Pod CPU/memory request and limit information

Certain information can be mounted into the pod as an environment variable, whereas other information can be accessed as files within a volume.

Table 5-1 outlines the metadata sources and how they can be accessed.

Table 5-1. Downward API sources

Item	Description	Environment variables	Volume
name	Pod name	Yes	Yes
namespace	Pod namespace	Yes	Yes
podIP	Pod IP address	Yes	No
labels	Labels attached to the pod	No	Yes
annotations	Annotations attached to the pod	No	Yes
resources	CPU and memory requests and limits	Yes	Yes

Utilizing the Downward API requires the addition of environment variables or volume mounts to the deployment configuration. The following pod spec gives an example of its usage:

```
kind: Pod
apiVersion: v1
metadata:
  labels:
    release: 'stable'
    environment: 'pre-prod'
    relationship: 'child'
    dmzbased: 'false'
    tier: 'front1'
  name: downward-api-pod
  annotations:
    example.com/skipValidation: 'true'
    example.com/MD5Checksum: '23798FGH'
    example.com/BUILDDATE: '3479845'
spec:
  containers:
    - name: volume-test-container
      image: gcr.io/google_containers/busybox
      command: ["sh", "-cx", "cat /etc/labels /etc/annotations;env"]
      volumeMounts:
        - name: podinfo
          mountPath: /etc
          readOnly: false
```

```
        env:
          - name: MIN_MEMORY
            valueFrom:
              resourceFieldRef:
                resource: requests.memory
          - name: MAX_MEMORY
            valueFrom:
              resourceFieldRef:
                resource: limits.memory
      volumes:
        - name: podinfo
          metadata:
            items:
              - name: "labels"
                fieldRef:
                  fieldPath: metadata.labels
              - name: "annotations"
                fieldRef:
                  fieldPath: metadata.annotations
      restartPolicy: Never
```

Using the preceding pod spec will result in the following output:

```
$ oc create -f metadata-pod.yaml

pod "downward-api-pod" created

$ oc logs downward-api-pod

+ cat /etc/labels /etc/annotations
dmzbased="false"
environment="pre-prod"
relationship="child"
release="stable"
tier="front1"example.com/BUILDDATE="3479845"
example.com/MD5Checksum="23798FGH"
example.com/skipValidation="true"
kubernetes.io/config.seen="2016-10-25T02:15:31.335189599-04:00"
kubernetes.io/config.source="api"
openshift.io/scc="restricted"
+ env
MIN_MEMORY=33554432
MAX_MEMORY=67108864
.
.
.
.
```

An example of use of this feature would be where the MAX_MEMORY and MIN_MEMORY
settings could be used to configure Java -Xmx -Xms memory settings in an application
startup script.

Handling Large Configuration Data Sets

Both secrets and configuration maps are stored in the underlying *etcd* data store within the OpenShift platform. For certain types of applications, configuration data may be hundreds of megabytes or larger in size, particularly for image-heavy applications or ones that consume a lot of binary data.

It's preferable to store configuration of that size outside of *etcd*. Two approaches which may help with this are persistent volumes and layered image builds.

Persistent Volumes

OpenShift supports stateful applications with persistent volumes (PVs) and persistent volume claims (PVCs). PVs are volumes backed by shared storage which are mounted into running pods. PVs can be backed by multiple different storage mechanisms (e.g., iSCSI, AWS EBS volumes, NFS, and others). PVCs are manifests that pods use to retrieve and mount the volume into the pod at initialization time. PVCs can have different types of access modes (i.e., ReadWriteOnce, ReadOnlyMany, ReadWrite-Many).

To handle large config files, one approach is to copy the configuration onto the PV and mount the storage into the relevant pods using a ReadOnlyMany access mode. Note, however, that any changes to the configuration files will not be detected by OpenShift so the pods will have to be manually restarted if required.

Layered Images

OpenShift supports a layered images approach to building images. A layered image is where the running image is made up of different *layers* where each layer sits on the binaries/data of the previous layer.

Most of the time this approach is used to provide a container standard operating environment (SOE) consisting of base operating system and application platform dependencies. It can also be extended to incorporate configuration data as well.

Used in conjunction with the previously discussed Downward API approach, configuration can be switched dynamically depending on the environment/namespace (Figure 5-3).

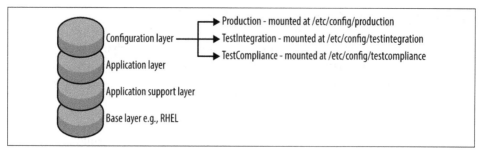

Figure 5-3. Layered image and Downward API

This approach has a number of advantages:

- There is a single artifact (image) which is managed.
- The image is stored in the registry.
- No *etcd* storage impact, so large amounts of configuration data can be stored in the image.

The disadvantages of this approach are as follows:

- The inflexibility to change and the need to perform image builds in order to modify configuration.
- Breaks the initial recommendation of not storing configuration with application image.

This approach could be used where the container contains both the application and associated internationalized help files or documentation which would be cumbersome to load by other methods; or where container images needed to be fully inclusive of configuration/content when being promoted between different OCP clusters (e.g., development and production where the two clusters are seperate with only a registry in common).

Summary

This chapter has demonstrated the multiple methods by which configuration can be managed in OpenShift. Each method can be used individually or in conjunction with other configuration methods depending on the configuration needs of the applications running in containers. The next chapter will discuss how to package applications into containers to run on OpenShift.

## CHAPTER 6

Custom Image Builds

In OpenShift a running application is simply one or more container images running in a pod. The mechanism by which the application is packaged into a runnable container image is called an image build.

OpenShift Builds

In OpenShift a *build* is the name given to the process of building a runnable container image.

The build process is concerned with extracting the application's source or binary artifacts from some source, compiling the code if required, and layering the runtime artifact onto a base image to run it.

Once built, the container image is uploaded to the OpenShift registry to be used in the deployment process.

Build Strategies

A *build strategy* is the approach used to build the runtime image.

OpenShift supports a number of build strategies:

Source-to-Image (S2I)
> The S2I uses the open source S2I tool to enable developers to reproducibly build images by layering the application's source or binary artifacts onto a container image. The developer has to provide the location of the artifact and the builder image to use.

Docker

The Docker strategy allows developers to build images by providing a Dockerfile containing Docker directives.

Pipeline

The Pipeline strategy uses the open source Jenkins continuous integration platform to build container images. The developer provides a Jenkinsfile containing the requisite build commands.

Custom

The custom strategy allows the developer to provide a customized builder image to build the runtime image.

Build Sources

The *source* is the location of the artifact used in the builder. Currently there are four sources, but not all sources are available to each strategy:

Git

The build configuration contains details of a Git-based repository from which the application's artifacts can be cloned.

Dockerfile

The build configuration contains an inline Dockerfile which is used to build the image.

Image

The build configuration references artifacts stored in other images. These artifacts are copied from the source images to the destination image as part of the build.

Binary

The artifact is streamed from a local filesystem to the builder.

Build Configurations

Builds are configured and controlled by build configuration resources. Build configurations contain the details of the chosen build strategy as well as the source of the developer-supplied artifacts such as Git location, the details of the builder image to be used, and the output image.

The following build configuration was created by running the command:

```
$ oc new-app https://github.com/openshift/nodejs-ex

[...output skipped...]

$ oc get bc/nodejs-ex -o yaml
```

```
apiVersion: v1
kind: BuildConfig
metadata:
  annotations:
    openshift.io/generated-by: OpenShiftNewApp
  creationTimestamp: 2017-01-30T21:18:02Z
  labels:
    app: nodejs-ex
  name: nodejs-ex
  namespace: test-project
  resourceVersion: "26555"
  selfLink: /oapi/v1/namespaces/test-project/buildconfigs/nodejs-ex
  uid: 9521be5e-e731-11e6-b3e5-eed674f91078
spec:
  nodeSelector: null
  output:
    to:
      kind: ImageStreamTag
      name: nodejs-ex:latest                              ❶
  postCommit: {}
  resources: {}
  runPolicy: Serial
  source:
    git:
      uri: https://github.com/openshift/nodejs-ex        ❷
    type: Git
  strategy:
    sourceStrategy:
      from:
        kind: ImageStreamTag
        name: nodejs:4                                    ❸
        namespace: openshift
    type: Source                                          ❹
  triggers:
  - github:
      secret: cMROkbapdsuPwt5IX6-d
    type: GitHub
  - generic:
      secret: ff-Nsmz2z45Isx29GknH
    type: Generic
  - type: ConfigChange
  - imageChange:
      lastTriggeredImageID: centos/nodejs-4-
centos7@sha256:f437d0de54a294d19f84d738e74dc1aef70403fbe479316018fb43edcdafbf92
    type: ImageChange
status:
  lastVersion: 1
```

Of interest is:

❶   The resultant image is output to `nodejs-ex:latest` in the OCP registry.

❷   The source code is retrieved from the master branch of the Git repository located at *https://github.com/openshift/nodejs-ex.git*.

❸   The builder image is `nodejs:4`.

❹   An S2I build strategy is being used.

Also notice that we did not specify the build image to use. This was *auto-magically* determined under the covers by the S2I executable during its introspection of the source files in the Git repo.

 Unless specified otherwise, the `oc new-app` command will scan the supplied Git repository. If it finds a Dockerfile, the *Docker* build strategy will be used; otherwise the *Source* strategy will be used and an S2I builder will be configured.

If the `oc new-app` command discovered a Dockerfile in the Git repository, then the build configuration would contain the following:

```
...
strategy:
  dockerStrategy:
    from:
      kind: ImageStreamTag
      name: centos:latest
  type: Docker
...
```

Creating build configs

Image builds can be created in either the OpenShift UI or via the CLI. You can do this in the CLI as follows:

```
$ oc new-build openshift/nodejs-010-centos7~https://github.com/openshift/nodejs-
ex.git
  --name='newbuildtest'
```

Alternatively, you can use this:

```
$ oc new-app openshift/nodejs-010-centos7~https://github.com/openshift/nodejs-
ex.git
  --name='newapptest'
```

`oc new-build` and `oc new-app` are somewhat similar in function. Both create build configurations and image streams. However, `oc new-app` creates additional Open‐Shift resources such as *services* and `DeploymentConfigs`.

Source to Image

When building and deploying multiple applications, one recommendation to take onboard is to limit the proliferation of multiple different build mechanisms being used by DevOps teams. This is also true when building applications on the OpenShift platform. An optimal approach is to have a set of image builders which are reused across the applications being deployed onto the platform.

OpenShift comes with a number of these out of the box (Figure 6-1).

Figure 6-1. OCP builder images

The main components of S2I-type builders are as follows:

Builder image
> This container image provides the installation and runtime dependencies for the application.

S2I scripts
> There are a number of S2I scripts:
>
> - assemble (required)—Process the injected artifact (e.g., compile or install onto the builder image).
> - run (required)—The script to start up the application.
> - usage (optional)—Print instructions on how to use the builder image.
> - save-artifacts (optional)—Stream dependencies to standard out. This can help improve the execution time of the build if incremental builds are supported by the builder image.
> - test/run (optional)—Verify if the image is working properly.

The builder image comes with a set of default S2I scripts provided by the author Builder image. These scripts can be changed by the application developer (see "Custom S2I Scripts" on page 83).

S2I Process

The S2I build process consists of the following steps:

1. Start an instance of the builder image.
2. Retrieve the source artifacts from the specified repository.
3. Place the source artifacts as well as the S2I scripts into the builder image. This is done by bundling them up into a tar file and streaming it into the builder image.
4. Execute the *assemble* script.
5. Commit the image and push it to the OCP registry as referenced by the *Image-Stream* definition in the build configuration.

> By default, the injected artifacts are placed in the */tmp* directory. This can be changed using the *io.openshift.s2i.destination* label on the builder image. Similarly, the location of the S2I scripts can be controlled by the *io.openshift.s2i.scripts-url* label.

OpenShift ships with a large number of builder images (e.g., NodeJS, Ruby, Python, Dot Net, and others). These builder images perform source builds in which they download the source code onto the builder, compile it, and then install the compiled source onto the destination image.

However, sometimes it is preferable to customize the image build process (e.g., place the application binaries in a specific location).

There are two methods to customize the build process:

- Custom S2I scripts
- Custom S2I builder

Custom S2I Scripts

Developers can provide their own S2I scripts (e.g., assemble, run, etc.) to use within the S2I build process, overwriting some if not all of the default scripts. By placing the scripts in the *.s2i/bin* directory at the base of their source code repository, the scripts will be injected into the builder image by the S2I process and used during the build and subsequent execution phases.

Build environment

The *.s2i* directory can also contain a file named *environment* which can be used to inject environment variables into the build process. An example of this would be to add custom settings to the build process. The format of the file is a simple *key=value* pair.

This can also be done by adding environment variables to the build configuration via the oc set env command. For example:

```
$ oc set env bc/myapp OPTIMIZE=true
```

Custom S2I Builder

It is also possible to write your own custom S2I builder with your own builder image and S2I scripts. We're going to build a very basic Java builder one as a demonstration of how to do this.

The custom S2I builder will perform the following actions:

1. Provide a customized runtime Java environment.
2. Retrieve an injected Java JAR file injected by the S2I process.

3. Copy the JAR file into a specific location to be executed by the run script.
4. Execute the run script.

 This example retrieves the binary artifact from a Git repository. While it is generally not recommended to store binary files in a source repository, this is done for illustration purposes only.

Builder Image

The image builder is basically a Dockerfile which installs the required dependencies to build and run the application:

```
FROM centos:latest                                          ❶
MAINTAINER noconnor@redhat.com

RUN yum install -y java wget mvn --setopt=tsflags=nodocs && \
    yum -y clean all                                        ❷

LABEL io.k8s.description="Platform for building and running Java8 apps" \
      io.k8s.display-name="Java8" \
      io.openshift.expose-services="8080:http" \
      io.openshift.tags="builder,java8" \
      io.openshift.s2i.destination="/opt/app" \
      io.openshift.s2i.scripts-url=image:///usr/local/s2i   ❸

RUN adduser --system -u 10001 javauser
RUN mkdir -p /opt/app  && chown -R javauser: /opt/app

COPY ./S2iScripts/ /usr/local/s2i

USER 10001
EXPOSE 8080                                                 ❹

CMD ["/usr/local/s2i/usage"]                                ❺
```

❶ The base image that will run the application.

❷ Required build and runtime dependencies.

❸ Labels used to describe the builder. These will be used to populate the categories in the OpenShift UI. See "S2I labels" on page 85.

❹ Port to expose to handle application traffic.

❺ The usage script to be run by default.

S2I labels

io.openshift.s2i.destination
The location where the S2I process will place the application artifacts (e.g., source code or binary files)

io.openshift.s2i.scripts-url
The location of the S2I scripts

There is also a set of image metadata labels (*http://red.ht/2nZ76qc*) that can help OpenShift manage the resource needs of the container.

S2I Scripts

Assemble

In our example, the *assemble* script just copies the injected application Java JAR file and moves it to the filesystem location expected by the *run* script. The script also renames the JAR file to *openshift-app.jar*.

 This image builder only supports binary builds and not source builds. However, this is easily changed and left as an exercise for the reader.

```
#!/bin/bash -e
#
# S2I assemble script for the 'book-custom-s2i' image.
# The 'assemble' script currently only supports binary builds.
#
# For more information refer to the documentation:
#    https://github.com/openshift/source-to-image/blob/master/docs/
builder_image.md
#
if [ ! -z ${S2I_DEBUG} ]; then
        echo "turning on assemble debug";
   set -x
fi

# Binary deployment is a single jar
if [ $(ls /opt/app/src/*.jar | wc -l) -eq 1 ]; then
   mv /opt/app/src/*.jar /opt/app/openshift-app.jar
else
   echo "Jar not found in /opt/app/src/"
   exit 1
fi
```

Run

The *run* script simply executes the Java JAR from where the *assemble* has placed it. The run script is configured as the default command on the resulting image.

```
#!/bin/bash -e
java ${JAVA_OPTS} -jar /opt/app/openshift-app.jar
```

The S2I build process is highly customizable and can cater for many kinds of build types and approaches. It would be very straightforward to build a custom S2I builder which retrieved runtime application artifacts as part of the application startup processing the *run* script. This should be avoided as it makes the artifact repository a runtime dependency and can complicate the rollback of applications if deployment errors occur. It is recommended that all application images be fully populated with the application binaries before being written to the registry by the S2I process.

Adding a New Builder Image

Build the builder image in the OpenShift namespace and store the image in the OpenShift Registry:

```
$ oc new-build https://github.com/devops-with-openshift/book-custom-s2i.git -n
openshift
```

By default, the builder image is only available in the project/namespace that it's created in. To make it available to all projects in the OpenShift cluster, install it in the *OpenShift* namespace. However, the default user doesn't have access to create images in the OpenShift namespace, so ensure that the user you're logged in as has these permissions (e.g., `oc login -u system:admin`).

Building a Sample Application

This example uses our installed builder to take a sample JAR file and deploy it onto OpenShift. A sample application is provided at *https://github.com/devops-with-openshift/ItemsWS* under the *app* directory.

- To create the project, run the following command:

```
$ oc new-project bookprj --description='Custom Builder Example' \
  --display-name='book project'
```

- To build the application using the *custom builder* and specifying the location within the GIT repository for the binary artifact:

```
$ oc new-app book-custom-s2i~https://github.com/devops-with-openshift/ItemsWS \
  --context-dir='app'
```

- Create the route:

```
$ oc expose service itemsws
```

- Get the exposed route:

```
$ oc get routes
NAME        HOST/PORT                                PATH    SERVICES   PORT
TERMINATION
itemsws     itemsws-bookprj.192.168.1.27.xip.io              itemsws    8080-tcp
```

Use a browser go to the exposed route—for example, *http://itemsws-bookprj. 192.168.1.27.xip.io/items.*

You should see something like Figure 6-2.

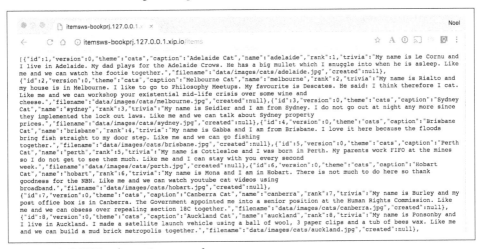

Figure 6-2. REST web service example

Alternative approach

It's also possible to use a *binary build* approach to build the application. In this example we assume that the sample application has been cloned from GitHub and is available on the developer's desktop.

This approach also assumes that the developer is working in the *bookprj2* project.

To set up the project, run the following commands:

```
$ oc new-project bookprj2
Now using project "bookprj2" on server "https://127.0.0.1:8443".

$cd /tmp
```

```
$git clone https://github.com/devops-with-openshift/ItemsWS
git clone https://github.com/devops-with-openshift/ItemsWS
Cloning into 'ItemsWS'...
remote: Counting objects: 67, done.
remote: Total 67 (delta 0), reused 0 (delta 0), pack-reused 67
Unpacking objects: 100% (67/67), done.
Checking connectivity... done.

$cd ItemsWS/app
$pwd
/tmp/ItemsWS/app
```

- Create the application build using the custom builder. Notice the --binary=true flag. This turns the build from a *source* build where source code is injected into the builder to a *binary* build where the compiled application is streamed into the builder image:

```
$ oc new-build --image-stream=book-custom-s2i --binary=true --name=test-app \
  --strategy=source

--> Found image ebff189 (9 minutes old) in image stream "openshift/book-custom-
s2i" under tag "latest" for "book-custom-s2i"

    Java8
    -----
    Platform for building and running Java8 applications

    Tags: builder, java8

    * A source build using binary input will be created
      * The resulting image will be pushed to image stream "test-app:latest"
      * A binary build was created, use 'start-build --from-dir' to trigger a
new build

--> Creating resources with label build=test-app ...
    imagestream "test-app" created
    buildconfig "test-app" created
--> Success
```

- Start the build. The *CLI* will automatically stream the referenced JAR file to the builder image as part of the *binary* build process:

```
$ oc start-build test-app --from-file=ItemWS-0.0.1-SNAPSHOT.jar
Uploading file "ItemWS-0.0.1-SNAPSHOT.jar" as binary input for the build ...
build "test-app-1" started
```

- Check for the built image:

```
$ oc get is
NAME        DOCKER REPO                             TAGS      UPDATED
test-app    172.30.197.150:5000/bookprj2/test-app   latest    About a minute ago
```

- Start the built image:

```
$ oc run test-app --image=172.30.197.150:5000/bookprj2/test-app
deploymentconfig "test-app" created
```

- Expose the route:

```
$ oc expose dc/test-app --port=8080
service "test-app" exposed

$ oc expose service/test-app
route "test-app" exposed
```

 It is also possible to deploy, run, and create the service by using the
oc new-app and oc expose commands.

```
$ oc new-app test-app

--> Found image 424d88c (7 minutes old) in image stream "bookprj2/test-app"
under tag "latest" for "test-app"

    bookprj2/test-app-1:88a4cf64
    ----------------------------
    Platform for building and running Java8 applications

    Tags: builder, java8

    * This image will be deployed in deployment config "test-app"
    * Port 8080/tcp will be load balanced by service "test-app"
      * Other containers can access this service through the hostname "test-app"

--> Creating resources ...
    deploymentconfig "test-app" created
    service "test-app" created
--> Success
    Run 'oc status' to view your app

$ oc expose svc/test-app

route "test-app" exposed
```

Troubleshooting

The image build logs can be viewed by either:

- Adding the --follow flag to the start-build command:

```
$ oc start-build test-app --from-file=ItemWS-0.0.1-SNAPSHOT.jar --follow
```

- Viewing the log files during or after the build:

```
$ oc get builds
NAME                TYPE      FROM      STATUS     STARTED        DURATION
test-app-1          Source    Binary    Complete   25 hours ago   5s
test-app-2          Source    Binary    Complete   25 hours ago   5s
test-app-3          Source    Binary    Complete   25 hours ago   5s

$ oc logs build/test-app-3
I0101 12:45:05.275821       1 builder.go:53] $BUILD env var is
{"kind":"Build","apiVersion":"v1","metadata":{"name":"test-
app-3","namespace":"test",.........
```

The S2I process also has different log levels that can be set by adding the BUILD_LOGLE
VEL environment variable to the build config:

```
$ oc set env bc/test-app BUILD_LOGLEVEL=5
```

The levels range from 0, which only outputs errors and *assemble* script output, to 5,
which includes detailed S2I and Docker information.

Troubleshooting the custom S2I scripts is also possible by adding a debug flag to the
scripts. In the sample script there is an environment variable S2I_DEBUG which turns
on bash tracing. This environment variable can be set by either:

- Adding a variable to the build configuration:

```
$ oc set env bc/test-app S2I_DEBUG=true
```

- Or by adding it in an *environment* file to the *.s2i* directory under the *apps* directory:

```
$cat ItemsWS/app/.s2i/environment
S2I_DEBUG=true
```

Summary

This chapter discussed builds and some of the multiple methods by which applications can be layered onto images. These concepts and examples will be useful to the
reader when customizing the OCP build process for their enviroment.

The custom S2I builder shown here is a very basic builder, and there are many
enhancements and features that can be used to make the builder more reliable and
enterprise-ready. For example:

- Handling secured artifact repositories with secrets
- Extended builds

- Using secrets
- Using build hooks
- Parallel builds

These and more are covered in the OpenShift documentation (*https://docs.open shift.com/*).

## CHAPTER 7

Application Management

In this chapter we are going to explore common management and monitoring tools, procedures, and practices when running and operating container workloads on OpenShift. This includes topics such as logging and metrics, as well as resource scheduling and how we can set quota and limits to help improve the utilization of compute resources across all the nodes in our OpenShift cluster.

To help understand the operational layers, we define three here:

Operating system infrastructure operations
    Deals with compute, network, storage, and operating systems

Cluster operations
    This is all about OpenShift and Kubernetes cluster management

Application operations
    Instrumenting and monitoring deployments, telemetry, logging, etc.

While we will focus on the third layer, in our DevOps world some of these concerns may in fact be carried out by developers with operational sensibilities!

Integrated Logging

The first place to look when troubleshooting software issues is normally in the log files. OpenShift provides access to logs for infrastructure, builds, deployments, and running applications. Container-based application architectures have multitiered logs that consist of container application logs, daemon logs, and general operating system logs.

Container Logs Are Transient

With transient containers, it is considered an anti-pattern to log to ephemeral storage within the container itself. Generally, the filesystem that the container mounts is recreated every time the container is (re)started. The following options are generally available for collecting the application container logs:

- Logging via data volumes
- Logging via the Docker logging driver
- Logging via a dedicated logging container
- Logging via the sidecar container approach

OpenShift provides integrated application logging via the Docker logging driver. In the latest versions of OpenShift, Docker is configured to use the systemd journal daemon `journald`. The Docker logging driver reads log events directly from the container's `STDOUT` and `STDERR` output. There are several benefits to this approach:

- Your containers do not need to write to and read from log files, resulting in performance gains.
- Log events are stored on the host machine and bypass the Docker log daemon.
- It allows you to enable node log rotation, and limit log size and rate.
- You can use `journalctl` to retrieve container logs.

Using `STDOUT` and `STDERR` convention means that you do not need to configure specific log files and directories within your applications. So if your application uses different log files for different things, you may need to add other log fields to differentiate these in your log stream.

Logs for your individual pods can be seen in the web-ui by navigating to Applications → Pods → Logs or by using the CLI:

```
oc logs -h
```

Aggregated Logging

The *EFK* stack aggregates logs from nodes and application pods running inside your OpenShift installation.

Elasticsearch
    An object store where all logs are stored, based on Lucene.

Fluentd
    Gathers logs from nodes and feeds them to Elasticsearch.

Kibana

A web-ui for Elasticsearch.

The EFK containers are normally deployed in a privileged OpenShift namespace by a cluster administrator.

 You will need to run `oc cluster up` using the `--logging=true` flag to enable the aggregated logging service.

It is also possible to integrate logging to external ES clusters or to use Fluentd secure forward to integrate into other logging solutions (such as Splunk, HDFS, or cloud-based logging solutions; see Figure 7-1).

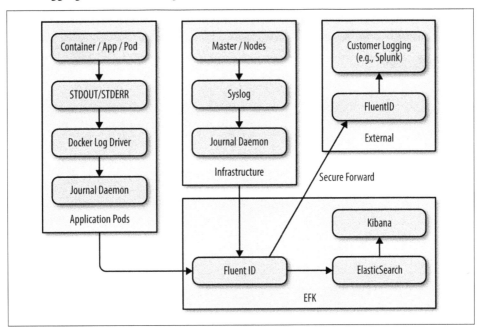

Figure 7-1. System, application, and external logs

Once deployed, Fluentd aggregates event logs from all nodes, projects, and pods into Elasticsearch (ES). It also provides a centralized Kibana web-ui where users and administrators can create rich visualizations and dashboards with the aggregated data.

Fluentd bulk uploads logs to an index, in JSON format, then Elasticsearch routes your search requests to the appropriate shards. Integrated role-based access control ensures that you may only view logs for projects and namespaces for which you have view or edit access. Cluster administrators can access all projects/namespace logs via Kibana.

Kibana

We are going to use the Cat/City of the Day application scaled up to two pods to explore some logging behavior with Kibana. When you drill down into a pod in the web-ui, and select the Logs → Archive Logs link, you will be directed to Kibana and get a default view for your pod logs (Figure 7-2).

Refer to the online documentation (*https://www.elastic.co/guide/en/kibana/4.1/ discover.html*) to understand Kibana basics.

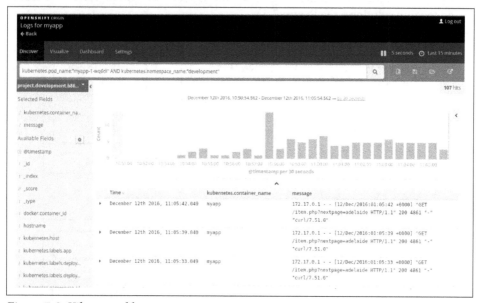

Figure 7-2. Kibana pod logs

Our application pod logs are annotated with OpenShift Kubernetes metadata by Fluentd. This is particularly useful for filtering in Kibana. By selecting a single log entry in Kibana, you can see all of the data types that are annotated with the log entry (Figure 7-3):

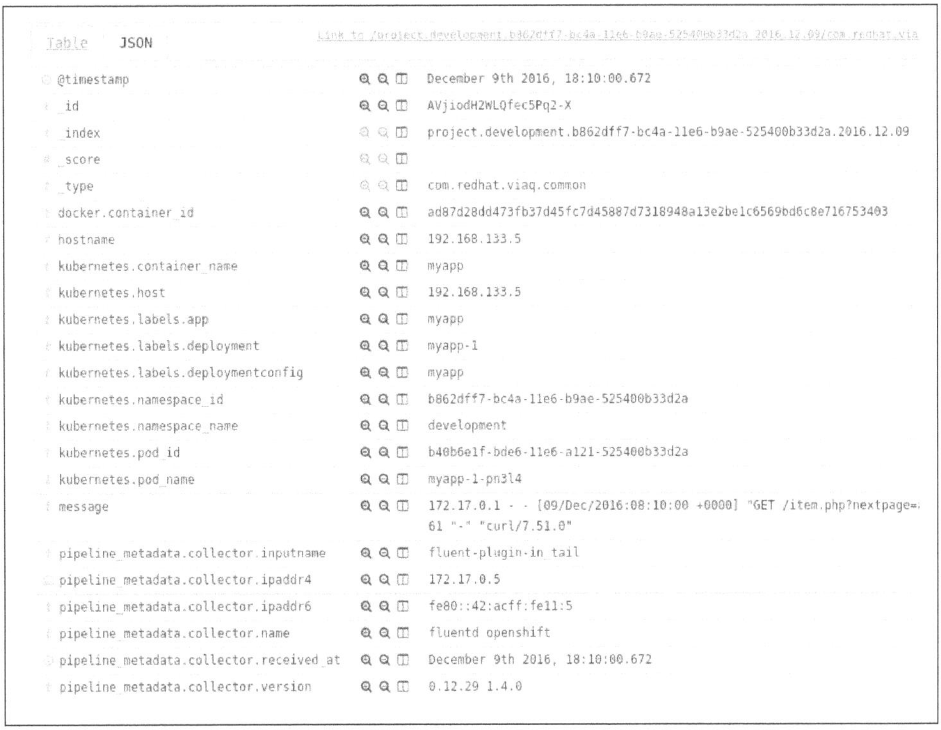

Figure 7-3. Single log entry with Kubernetes annotations

We may add a filter, create searches using the filter predicates, as well as save the searches for later use. OpenShift makes Kubernetes metadata available in the records so it can be used in the search for data. The time range can be changed in the upper-right corner of the Kibana Discover view.

Some General Aggregated Kibana Queries

Let's take a look at some common queries. We have defined a filter for the project name *kubernetes.namespace_name: "development"* shown in green in the following examples:

- What are all the logs, for the last hour, for a *single version* of a single application in my project, but across all replicas (Figure 7-4)?

```
kubernetes_labels_deployment:"<name of replication controller>"
```

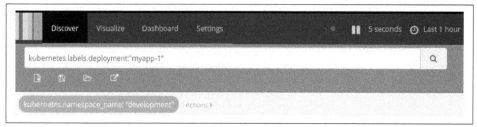

Figure 7-4. Single application, single version, last hour search

- What are all the logs, for the last hour, for *all versions* of a single application in my project, but across all replicas (Figure 7-5)?

```
kubernetes_labels_deployment:"<name of deployment configuration>"
```

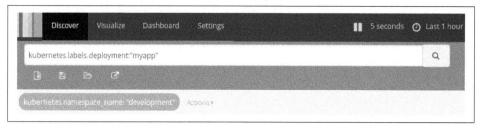

Figure 7-5. Single application, all versions, last hour search

- What are all the logs, categorized as error, for the last hour for all versions of a single application in my project, but across all replicas (Figure 7-6)?

```
kubernetes_labels_deployment:"<name of deployment configuration>" &&
mesasge:"error"
```

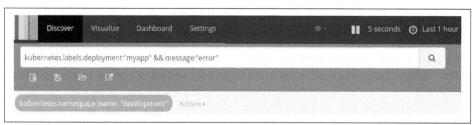

Figure 7-6. Single application, all versions, errors last hour search

Simple Metrics

With cluster metrics (*http://red.ht/2oD9fLj*) deployed, OpenShift provides memory, CPU, and network bandwidth metrics for individual pods, and aggregated for all pod replicas.

> You will need to run `oc cluster up` using the `--metrics=true` flag to enable the metrics service.

As shown in Figure 7-7, you can also drill down into individual pods to see graphical views that may be viewed over different time ranges.

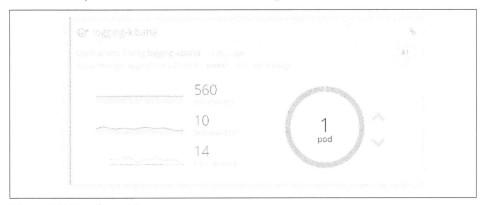

Figure 7-7. Simple metrics

The kubelet on each OpenShift node exposes metrics that can be collected and stored in backends by Heapster. As an OpenShift Container Platform administrator, you can view a cluster's metrics from all containers and components in one user interface.

These metrics are also used by horizontal pod autoscalers in order to determine when and how to scale. If resource limits are defined for your project, then you can also see a donut chart for each pod. Hawkular Metrics stores the data persistently (if configured) in a Cassandra database.

It is also possible to query the Hawkular metric API endpoint directly. Some very useful resources include:

- The upstream documentation for metrics (*https://github.com/openshift/origin-metrics/blob/master/docs/hawkular_metrics.adoc*)

- Hawkular REST endpoint documentation (*http://www.hawkular.org/docs/rest/rest-metrics.html*)

- Heapster schema documentation (*https://github.com/kubernetes/heapster/blob/master/docs/storage-schema.md*)

To query metrics, set the HTTP headers shown in Table 7-1 on the request.

Table 7-1. Hawkular HTTP query headers

Header	Description	Value
Content-Type	The desired return content type	application/json;charset=UTF-8
Hawkular-Tenant	The name of your OpenShift project	development
Authorization	The token returned by oc whoami -t or a service account token	Bearer L1D7XYL0oZk2v_ZuHKCZ3HUBkpu_AqlkvNV4VeAx_EY

So, to retrieve all of the metrics being held (not the raw data) for our *development* project, we can use:

```
$ curl -k -X GET -H 'Content-Type: application/json;charset=UTF-8' \
    -H 'Hawkular-Tenant: development' \
    -H "Authorization: Bearer L1D7XYL0oZk2v_ZuHKCZ3HUBkpu_AqlkvNV4VeAx_EY" \
    'https://metrics-openshift-infra.192.168.133.5.xip.io/hawkular/metrics/
metrics'
```

You will see that each metric being collected has an *ID* that we can then use to query the raw data. Let's try and query one of these *ID*s. Looking at the Heapster Schema documentation we can see that the uptime field refers to the *number of milliseconds since the container was started*. So we can query the raw uptime data for a pod using the *ID* listed in the preceding output as follows:

```
$ curl -k -X GET -H 'Content-Type: application/json;charset=UTF-8' \
    -H 'Hawkular-Tenant: development' \
    -H "Authorization: Bearer L1D7XYL0oZk2v_ZuHKCZ3HUBkpu_AqlkvNV4VeAx_EY" \
    https://metrics-openshift-infra.192.168.133.5.xip.io/hawkular/metrics/coun-
ters/pod%2Fde6e8516-c024-11e6-9789-525400b33d2a%2Fuptime/data
...
  {
    "timestamp": 1481517550000,
    "value": 26478
  },
  {
    "timestamp": 1481517540000,
    "value": 15950
  }
...
```

Replace / for URL encoded %2F characters in the metric *ID* portion of the query at the end of the GET request. For example:

```
original id: pod/de627da6-c024-11e6-9789-525400b33d2a/
uptime
query string: pod%2Fde6e8516-c024-11e6-9789-525400b33d2a
%2Fuptime
```

You can also combine a visualization layer such as *Grafana* to build custom and dynamic dashboards on top of Hawkular metrics. There are some great blog posts (*http://bit.ly/2obs2MJ*) that show you how to do this.

Resource Scheduling

For end users, the default OpenShift configuration provides a seemingly infinite pool of cluster resources (compute, memory, networking) that can be consumed at will when developing, testing, and deploying applications.

Of course, cluster administrators have to manage and allocate resources across projects, otherwise users (over time) will most certainly consume all available cluster resources! As a developer, you can also set requests and limits on compute resources at the pod and container level.

It is important for users to understand resource requests and limits so that no one team uses more than its fair share of resources.

If you do not specify what resources you need, what is OpenShift's default behavior?

- You get *Best Effort* isolation (i.e., no promises about what resources can be allocated for your project).
- You might get *defaulted* values (i.e., this depends on cluster and/or project/namespace default configuration).
- You might get *Out Of Memory* killed randomly (e.g., if the node your workload is running on runs out of resources).
- You might get *CPU starved* (e.g., it might take five minutes to schedule your workload).

If you are running a development pod or some low-priority workload, the default behavior might be OK. Of course, if it's production you definitely need to think about what resources your project needs. Common questions include:

- How many replicas does my workload need?
- How much CPU/memory does my workload need over a period of time?
- Should you provision for *mission-critical* worst-case scenarios (wasteful?)?

- Should you provision for average *over-commit* use cases (and have a higher failure rate?)?
- Should you provision for *high density, high quality of service* (burstable?)?

At its core, the Kubernetes scheduler is built around the concept of managing CPU and memory resources at a container level. Every OpenShift node is assigned an amount of schedulable memory and CPU. Every container has a choice of how much memory and CPU it will request. And the scheduler finds the best fit given the allocated CPU and memory on the nodes.

There are two basic concepts involved in tuning behavior:

- The *request* value specifies the minimum value you will be guaranteed. This corresponds to CPU shares with CGroups and is used to determine which containers should get killed first when a system is running out of memory. The request value is also used by the scheduler to assign pods to nodes. So a node is considered available if it can satisfy the requests of all the containers in a pod.
- The *limit* value specifies the max value you can consume. This corresponds to a CGroup CPU quota and memory limit, in bytes. Limit is the value applications should be tuned to use.

Put another way, *requests* are used for scheduling your container and provide a minimum service guarantee. *Limits* constrain the amount of compute resources that may be consumed on your node.

The scheduler attempts to improve utilization of your compute resources across all nodes in your cluster by using a policy to best fit your application containers on each node.

Getting accurate benchmarks for your applications can be extremely hard for complicated distributed systems. Resource needs will change over time. Currently, scheduling is based on requested values, and there is some hit and miss in figuring out what these should be for your applications.

At a minimum you will need to decide on the quality of service characteristics your applications require for CPU/RAM:

Best-Effort

A request value of 0 (unlimited) with *no limit* set is classified as best effort. Best-Effort containers are the first to get killed when resources are limited.

Guaranteed

A container with a *request value equal to its limit*. These containers will never get killed based on resource constraints.

`Burstable`

A container with a *request value less than its limit*. Will be killed after `Best-Effort` containers when resources are limited if their usage exceeds their request value.

Let's have a look at controls you may consider for your workloads.

Quotas

The code configuration examples for the following sections can also be found on GitHub (*http://bit.ly/AppManConfigs*).

You can create resources using `oc create -f <URL to raw file>`.

Resource quotas let you specify how much memory and CPU your project can consume. They provide *hard* constraints that limit aggregate resource consumption per project.

Quotas can limit the quantity of objects that can be created in a project, as well as the total amount of compute resources that may be consumed by resources in that project. The product documentation (*http://red.ht/2nFhe5A*) provides great information.

Let's add some quotas (hard limits) to a project named *development* (go ahead and create a new project if necessary):

```
$ oc login -u developer -p developer
$ oc new-project development --display-name='Development' \
    --description='Development'
```

As a cluster admin user, create a quota based on OpenShift object counts. You may specify some or all of these object types:

```
$ oc login -u system:admin
$ oc create -n development -f - <<EOF
apiVersion: v1
kind: ResourceQuota
metadata:
  name: core-object-counts
spec:
  hard:
    pods: "4" ❶
    configmaps: "5" ❷
    persistentvolumeclaims: "2" ❸
    replicationcontrollers: "10" ❹
    resourcequotas: "4" ❺
    secrets: "10" ❻
    services: "5" ❼
```

```
    openshift.io/imagestreams: "10" ❽
EOF
```

❶ The total number of pods that can exist in the project.

❷ The total number of ConfigMap objects that can exist in the project.

❸ The total number of persistent volume claims (PVCs) that can exist in the
    project.

❹ The total number of replication controllers that can exist in the project.

❺ The total number of resource quotas that can exist in the project.

❻ The total number of secrets that can exist in the project.

❼ The total number of services that can exist in the project.

❽ The total number of image streams that can exist in the project.

We may then query these as any user (or view them in the web-ui under the Resources → Quota tab):

```
$ oc describe quota -n development

Name:                          core-object-counts
Namespace:                     development
Resource                       Used       Hard
--------                       ----       ----
configmaps                     0          5
openshift.io/imagestreams      0          5
persistentvolumeclaims         0          2
pods                           0          4
replicationcontrollers         0          10
resourcequotas                 1          4
secrets                        9          10
services                       0          5
```

Now let's add some compute resource quotas:

```
$ oc login -u system:admin
$ oc create -n development -f - <<EOF
apiVersion: v1
kind: ResourceQuota
metadata:
  name: compute-resources
spec:
  hard:
    pods: "4" ❶
    requests.cpu: "0.2" ❷
```

```
        requests.memory: 1Gi ❸
        limits.cpu: "0.2" ❹
        limits.memory: 1Gi ❺
EOF
```

❶ The total number of pods in a nonterminal state that can exist in the project.

❷ Across all pods in a nonterminal state, the sum of CPU requests cannot exceed 0.2 core.

❸ Across all pods in a nonterminal state, the sum of memory requests cannot exceed 1Gi.

❹ Across all pods in a nonterminal state, the sum of CPU limits cannot exceed 0.2 cores.

❺ Across all pods in a nonterminal state, the sum of memory limits cannot exceed 1Gi.

We can see these new quotas in the description:

```
$ oc describe quota -n development

Name:            compute-resources
Namespace:       development
Resource         Used      Hard
--------         ----      ----
limits.cpu       0         200m
limits.memory    0         1Gi
pods             1         4
requests.cpu     0         200m
requests.memory  0         1Gi
...
```

Quota Scopes

Each quota can have an associated set of *scopes*. A quota will only measure usage for a resource if it matches the listed scopes.

This can be useful if you wish to exclude or include build or deployment pods in your quotas (by setting scope to `NotTerminating` or `Terminating`) or for matching pods that are `BestEffort` for CPU and memory.

For example, to limit *pods* to one in our project for all pods that are `BestEffort` (i.e., have no *limit* or *requests* quotas set):

```
$ oc login -u system:admin
$ oc create -n development -f - <<EOF
apiVersion: v1
kind: ResourceQuota
```

```
metadata:
  name: besteffort
spec:
  hard:
    pods: "1"
  scopes:
  - BestEffort
EOF
```

By setting the Quota Scope to NotTerminating, for example, we can avoid deployment pod resources (see Chapter 3) from being counted as consumed resources.

Quota Enforcement

Once you create a quota, it is enforced when any new resource request is made. Usage stats for the project are calculated periodically, and upon creation or modification of quotas, the stats and limits are updated. New resource requests are restricted if limited by hard quota restraints:

```
$ oc login -u developer -p developer
$ oc project development
$ oc new-app --name=myapp \
    openshift/php:5.6~https://github.com/devops-with-openshift/cotd.git#master
$ oc expose --name=myapp \
    --hostname=cotd-development.192.168.137.3.xip.io \
    service myapp
```

What happened? No pods were created. Let's examine the project's event stream:

```
$ oc get events
...
2s          11s         22          myapp-1   Build                   Warning
FailedCreate        {build-controller }   Error creating: pods "myapp-1-build"
is forbidden: Failed quota: compute-resources: must specify limits.cpu,lim-
its.memory,requests.cpu,requests.memory
...
```

We can see the build pod is forbidden now that our cluster admin has specified project-based quotas. We need to specify values on our resources for CPU or memory. We can specify individual values in the *deployment config* or by setting project default values using limit ranges.

Limit Ranges and Requests Versus Limits

A LimitRange is a mechanism for specifying default project CPU and memory limits and requests. If a resource does not set an explicit value, and if the constraint supports a default value, then the default value is applied to the resource.

Let's define some default limits for our project as the cluster admin user:

```
$ oc login -u system:admin
$ oc create -n development -f - <<EOF
apiVersion: "v1"
kind: "LimitRange"
metadata:
  name: "core-resource-limits"
spec:
  limits:
    - type: "Pod"
      max:
        cpu: "0.2"
        memory: "1Gi"
      min:
        cpu: "50m"
        memory: "6Mi"
    - type: "Container"
      max:
        cpu: "2"
        memory: "1Gi"
      min:
        cpu: "50m"
        memory: "4Mi"
      default:
        cpu: "50m"
        memory: "200Mi"
      defaultRequest:
        cpu: "50m"
        memory: "100Mi"
      maxLimitRequestRatio:
        cpu: "10"
EOF
```

The limits are specified by pod and container, specifying min/max and default CPU/memory amounts. Our build pod should now run based on the default limits:

```
$ oc get pods

NAME            READY    STATUS     RESTARTS   AGE
myapp-1-build   1/1      Running    0          4s
```

We can examine the limits for our project:

```
$ oc get limits -n development
NAME                  AGE
core-resource-limits  1m

$ oc describe limits core-resource-limits -n development
Name:      core-resource-limits
Namespace: development
Type        Resource   Min   Max   Def Req   Def Lim   Max Lim/Req Ratio
---         --------   ---   ---   -------   -------   -----------------
Pod         memory     6Mi   1Gi   -         -         -
Pod         cpu        50m   200m  -         -         -
```

```
Container  memory   4Mi  1Gi  100Mi   200Mi    -
Container  cpu      50m  2    50m     50m      10
```

as well as visualize the project quota metrics in the web-ui (Figure 7-8).

Figure 7-8. Quota and limits

Multiproject Quotas

Up till now we have been looking at per-project quotas. It is also possible to create quotas across projects, or multiproject quotas. You may use project labels or annotations when creating these multiproject spanning quotas. For example, let's create a *pod* quota for our *developer* user across all their projects:

```
$ oc login -u system:admin
$ oc create clusterquota for-user-developer \
    --project-annotation-selector openshift.io/requester=developer \
    --hard pods=8
```

Normal users may then read and display this cluster quota:

```
$ oc login -u developer -p developer
$ oc describe AppliedClusterResourceQuota

Name:              for-user-developer
Namespace:         <none>
Created:           35 seconds ago
Labels:            <none>
Annotations:       <none>
Label Selector:    <null>
AnnotationSelector: map[openshift.io/requester:developer]
Resource      Used      Hard
---           ---       ---
pods          6         8
```

Applications

As a developer, you may need to make some changes to your application to have it properly adjust to the size of the container it's in. You can read the CGroup limit from within your container and adjust accordingly. If you are a Java developer, for example, you may dynamically set the MaxHeap parameter to a percentage of this value:

```
CONTAINER_MEMORY_IN_BYTES=`cat /sys/fs/cgroup/memory/memory.limit_in_bytes`

e.g.
$ oc exec myapp-1-ngadr cat /sys/fs/cgroup/memory/memory.limit_in_bytes
209715200
```

It is also possible to use the Kubernetes downward API to inject this value into your applications environment:

```
env:
  - name: MEMORY_LIMIT
    valueFrom:
      resourceFieldRef:
        resource: limits.memory
```

By rightsizing your application memory requirements dynamically, you will be much better placed to avoid out-of-memory events.

Eviction and Pod Rescheduling

Nodes may become unstable if all of the memory and compute resources become used up by your application workloads.

Normally on Linux, when system memory (RAM) becomes low, swap space is used instead. Swap space normally consists of a dedicated partition or file which is a lot slower for read/writes than physical RAM.

OpenShift provides a mechanism using eviction policies, so that a node can proactively monitor for and prevent against total starvation of a compute resource. To take advantage of memory-based evictions, OpenShift operators must disable swap:

```
$ swapoff -a
```

This allows pods to be evicted from a node when it is under memory pressure, and rescheduled on an alternative node that has no such pressure. Eviction policies are configured in the *node_config.yaml* file (these can also be set using Ansible). Both soft limits (based on grace period) and hard limits (if met eviction occurs) are supported.

For details on how to configure eviction policy, see the product documentation (*http://red.ht/2oExcS8*).

Overcommit

In nonproduction-type environments (where guaranteed performance is not a concern), operators may configure *overcommit* of compute resources.

Scheduling is based on resources requested, while quotas and hard limits refer to resource limits, which can be set higher than requested resources. The difference between request and limit determines the level of overcommit.

A node is overcommitted when it has a pod scheduled that makes no request, or when the sum of limits across all pods on that node exceeds available machine capacity.

For details on how to configure overcommit in your environment, see the product documentation (*http://red.ht/2nFsdMo*).

Auto Pod Scaling

As well as adjusting the number of pods by manually scaling a deployment configuration and/or a replication controller's `replicas` value, OpenShift provides more advanced scaling alternatives based on cluster metrics.

The first of these is based on the `HorizontalPodAutoscaler` (HPA) object. OpenShift automatically increases or decreases the scale of a replication controller or deployment configuration, based on metrics collected from the pods that belong to that replication controller or deployment configuration.

Cluster Metrics and Quota and Limits must be enabled for HPA to work.

The following metric is supported: CPU Utilization - Percentage of the requested CPU.

Autoscaling applies only to the latest deployment in the *Complete* phase.

See the product documentation (*http://red.ht/2nLR3ep*).

Use the following command to create an HPA for our application deployment:

```
$ oc autoscale dc myapp --min 1 --max 4 --cpu-percent=75
```

The min/max pods are the number of replicas to scale up and down to.

The `--cpu-percent` argument is the percentage of the requested CPU that each pod should ideally be using.

After an HPA is created, it begins attempting to query Heapster for metrics on the pods. It may take a few minutes before Heapster obtains the initial metrics (*<waiting>* will be displayed).

Eventually you will see a percentage in the CURRENT column:

```
$ oc get hpa myapp

NAME     REFERENCE                TARGET   CURRENT   MINPODS   MAXPODS   AGE
myapp    DeploymentConfig/myapp   75%      0%        1         4         2m
```

We can use a tool to generate traffic for our web application—for example, the Apache server benchmarking tool **ab** allows us to make 2,000 requests with 1,000 concurrently (you may need to adjust these for your environment):

```
$ while true; do ab -n 2000 -c 1000 \
    -k http://myapp-development.192.168.133.3.xip.io/item.php; sleep 0.5; done
```

As the CPU utilization increases as load builds up on our pod, we can watch the HPA as it scales up pods, in this case eventually reaching three pods (Figure 7-9):

```
$ while true; do oc get hpa/myapp; sleep 5; done

NAME     REFERENCE                TARGET   CURRENT   MINPODS   MAXPODS   AGE
myapp    DeploymentConfig/myapp   75%      0%        1         4         2m
myapp    DeploymentConfig/myapp   75%      38%       1         4         5m
myapp    DeploymentConfig/myapp   75%      62%       1         4         6m
myapp    DeploymentConfig/myapp   75%      94%       1         4         15m  ❶
myapp    DeploymentConfig/myapp   75%      68%       1         4         24m
myapp    DeploymentConfig/myapp   75%      88%       1         4         30m  ❷
myapp    DeploymentConfig/myapp   75%      68%       1         4         1h
```

❶ Scale up to two pods.

❷ Scale up to three pods.

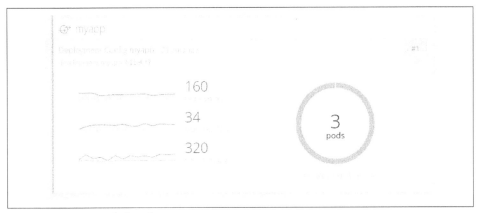

Figure 7-9. HPA scaled pods

If we examine the quotas and limits in the web-ui, we should also see the corresponding CPU and memory request increases, as shown in Figure 7-10.

Figure 7-10. HPA quota and limits

 You may have to adjust the ResourceQuota *compute-resources* up or down, or adjust the 75% HPA target to suit your environment to see HPA in action if the %current utilization does not reach the target.

Future releases of OpenShift will make more metrics available as well as provide different objects other than HPA for autoscaling workloads.

Java-Based Application Monitoring and Management Using Jolokia

When instrumenting Java applications that run in a JEE application server or within a JEE web server, a standard approach is to expose metrics via JMX (Java Management Extensions). Managed Beans (or MBeans) expose resource metrics for all manner of things, and you can, of course, create custom MBeans to instrument your own application-specific attributes.

Jolokia (*https://jolokia.org/documentation.html*) is an open source Java agent that implements a JMX-HTTP bridge, so you can easily query JMX resources over HTTP.

Jolokia has some great features, including multiplatform support, fine-grained security policies, and bulk requesting.

All of the standard Java xPaaS builder images provided for OpenShift integrate the Jolokia agent as standard and expose the Jolokia agent on port 8778 in your containers using the command line:

```
$ java -javaagent:/opt/jolokia/jolokia.jar=config=/opt/jolokia/etc/jolokia.prop-
erties ...
```

OpenShift provides an API proxy that allows you to securely connect to the Jolokia agent running in your container. Let's create a SpringBoot camel application using the OpenShift xPaaS Java S2I builder image so we can look at metrics in some more detail.

First, make sure you have the SpringBoot camel template loaded as a cluster admin:

```
$ oc login -u system:admin
$ BASEURL=https://raw.githubusercontent.com/jboss-fuse/application-templates/
application-templates-2.0.fuse-000027
$ oc replace --force -n openshift \
    -f ${BASEURL}/quickstarts/springboot-camel-template.json
```

Then create the application using S2I and the template as a normal user:

```
$ oc login -u developer -p developer
$ oc new-project spring-boot-cxf-jaxrs --display-name="spring-boot-cxf-jaxrs" \
    --description="spring-boot-cxf-jaxrs"
$ oc new-app --template=s2i-springboot-camel \
    -p GIT_REPO="https://github.com/fabric8-quickstarts/spring-boot-cxf-
jaxrs.git" \
    -p GIT_REF=""
$ oc expose dc s2i-springboot-camel --port=8080 --generator=service/v1
$ oc expose svc s2i-springboot-camel
```

Because this is a REST web service example application, we created a route so we can call the web service externally:

```
$ curl http://s2i-springboot-camel-spring-boot-cxf-jaxrs.192.168.137.3.xip.io/
services/helloservice/sayHello/mike

Hello mike, Welcome to CXF RS Spring Boot World!!!
```

Once the build has completed successfully, the running pod will expose the Jolokia port which we can see if we drill down in the web-ui (Figure 7-11).

Figure 7-11. Jolokia port

Rather handily, OpenShift also creates a link to *Open Java Console*. If you click on this, the hawt.io web console opens and shows you the JMX Attribute view as exposed by the Jolokia agent. Hawt.io allows you to manage and display all sorts of Java things, so check it out if you haven't seen it before.

We can connect to Jolokia from the CLI just like hawt.io does, with the following information:

```
$ OAUTH_TOKEN=`oc whoami -t`  ❶
$ MASTER_HOST=192.168.137.3  ❷
$ POD_NAME=`oc get pods -l app=s2i-springboot-camel -o name`  ❸
$ PROJECT_NAME=`oc project -q`  ❹
```

❶ OAuth token for the logged-in user.

❷ Master API endpoint for the OpenShift cluster.

❸ Application pod name from `oc get pods`.

❹ Project name from `oc project`.

We can query the Jolokia agent via the OpenShift proxy by doing:

```
$ curl -k -H "Authorization: Bearer $OAUTH_TOKEN" \
    https://$MASTER_HOST:8443/api/v1/namespaces/$PROJECT_NAME/pods/https:
$POD_NAME:8778/proxy/jolokia/
```

To return metrics for JMX attributes exposed by MBeans, we need to know the name of the attribute we are querying. You can find this easily in the hawt.io web-ui by selecting the JMX attribute object name—for example, the Java Heap Memory for our running application (Figure 7-12).

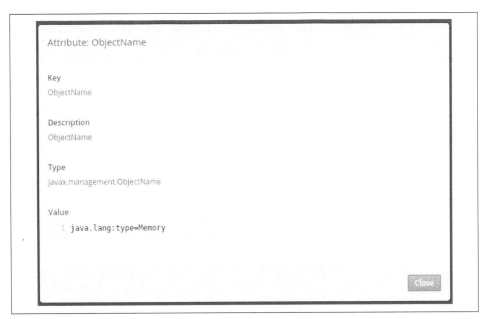

Figure 7-12. JMX Java Heap Memory

Let's read this variable using the CLI:

```
$ curl -k -H "Authorization: Bearer $OAUTH_TOKEN" \
    https://$MASTER_HOST:8443/api/v1/namespaces/$PROJECT_NAME/pods/https:
$POD_NAME:8778/proxy/jolokia/read/java.lang:type=Memory/HeapMemoryUsage
...
{
  "request": {
    "mbean": "java.lang:type=Memory",
    "attribute": "HeapMemoryUsage",
    "type": "read"
  },
  "value": {
    "init": 79691776,
    "committed": 458227712,
    "max": 1118830592,
    "used": 223657152
  },
  "timestamp": 1482884436,
  "status": 200
}
...
```

Let's say we are also interested in the HTTP request count and total thread count in our application. How can we query for all these?

Object Name	Attribute	Description
java.lang:type=Memory	HeapMemoryUsage	Java Heap Memory usage
java.lang:type=Threading	ThreadCount	Java Total Thread Count
Tomcat:type=RequestProcessor,worker="http-nio-0.0.0.0-8080",name=HttpRequest1	requestCount	HTTP Request count for application

We could easily create a custom chart of these, as shown in Figure 7-13 (see *https://github.com/devops-with-openshift/ose-jolokia-demo*).

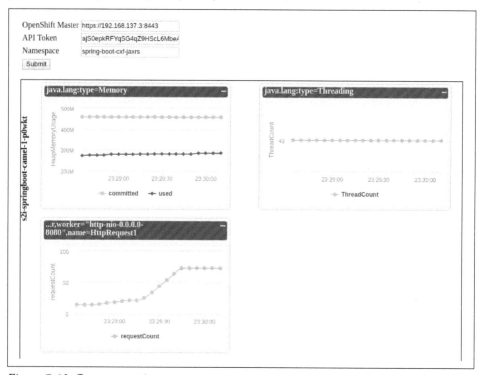

Figure 7-13. Custom metrics

Summary

In this chapter we looked at common application operational features of the Open-Shift platform. Integrated logging and metrics provide a first line of defense when troubleshooting application issues. By specifying resource limits and quotas against your projects, OpenShift can effectively schedule containers across your cluster, giving superior utilization with the quality of service level your business demands.

For advanced application metrics and monitoring, see:

- Hawkular APM (*https://hawkular.gitbooks.io/hawkular-apm-user-guide*)
- Hawkular Openshift Agent (*https://github.com/hawkular/hawkular-openshift-agent*)
- Prometheus (*https://prometheus.io*)
- Jolokia documentation (*https://jolokia.org/documentation.html*) (includes the full set of requests and responses that can be sent to Jolokia)

Afterword

We hope you have found this book to be a useful primer on how to build out an automated DevOps platform using OpenShift. There is so much to cover within OpenShift alone, so we deliberately chose to highlight a few critical, high-impact capabilities native to the platform.

When you come to apply this in your own environment, there is no doubt you will be integrating OpenShift with other tools as part of your broader organization-wide automation strategy. And again, while we have remained framework agnostic and language polyglot, you may be thinking in terms of a specific framework or language.

OpenShift is a dynamic and vibrant open source community project, so it plays well with other productivity tools, especially those sharing a common open community ethos. OpenShift Commons (*https://commons.openshift.org/*) is one place where we freely and openly gather many of these like minds. Some of you may be interested in the fabric8 project (*https://fabric8.io/*), which is building out an integrated end-to-end development platform for cloud native applications and microservices.

What We Covered

We encourage everyone to regularly check the OpenShift community for the exciting updates coming your way. Now let's recap what we covered over the course of the book:

- DevOps as value delivery and why it is important for DevOps automation-related tooling to be accessible and inclusive to participants of all skill sets in the software delivery process.

- Setting up your own local OpenShift cluster instance and so giving you full Developer, Operations, and Administration privileges to experiment and test OpenShift capabilities.

- Patterns and practical examples of how to do cloud-scale deployments such as rolling, A/B, blue-green, and canary using OpenShift, including an explanation of deployment configuration trigger behavior and lifecycle hooks.

- Coverage of OpenShift's native support for Jenkins, with guided examples on how to implement continuous integration pipelines, as well as how to integrate to third-party CI/CD automation tool chains using Git repository webhooks and related techniques.

- The different approaches to configuration management, including how to work with secrets and configmaps, and the use of labels and annotations and the downward API.

- A review of the source-to-image feature so that you can then build your own custom image build routines.

- A container nuanced view of application management functions, including log aggregation, metrics, and quota management.

- And finally, summing up many of the OpenShift concepts covered through the lens of the 12 Factor methodology.

Final Words

With OpenShift we are trying to help everyone do extraordinary things, making it safe and easy for all the participants to work together to quickly deliver great software that can make a real difference to users.

OpenShift is on its own journey of continuous innovation, absorbing feedback from the community users and contributors. Expect to see over time an expansion of the workload use cases covered by the OpenShift Container Management Platform. Emerging standards in the container and orchestration open source community projects will see more and more tools, services, and frameworks become first-class citizens of the platform.

Visit the OpenShift website (*https://www.openshift.com/*) and blog (*https://blog.open shift.com/*) for the latest and greatest features. If you have suggestions or want to provide feedback for the platform, talk to us via the various channels listed on the website project. But for now, stop reading and start coding!

OpenShift and 12 Factor Apps

12 Factor Apps is a methodology that outlines rules guiding application developers on how to build *cloud native* applications. The initial list came out of Heroku based on their experience running applications on their Heroku platform.

We strongly recommend that the readers become familiar with these *12 factors* and use them as a guide while implementing their application. They are described in detail at *https://12factor.net*. The 12 factors are:

Codebase
　　One codebase tracked in revision control, many deploys

Dependencies
　　Explicitly declare and isolate dependencies

Config
　　Store config in the environment

Backing services
　　Treat backing services as attached resources

Build, release, run
　　Strictly separate build and run stages

Processes
　　Execute the app as one or more stateless processes

Port binding
　　Export services via port binding

Concurrency
　　Scale out via the process model

Disposability
> Maximize robustness with fast startup and graceful shutdown

Dev/prod parity
> Keep development, staging, and production as similar as possible

Logs
> Treat logs as event streams

Admin processes
> Run admin/management tasks as one-off processes

We have also extended the list to include:

Security
> DevSecOps allows seamless collaboration between teams to effectively mitigate risk using a defense in-depth ecosystem approach

The purpose of this appendix is to go through each of the factors and map how they apply to application development using the OpenShift Container Platform.

Codebase

"A twelve-factor app is always tracked in a version control system... A codebase is any single repo (in a centralized revision control system like Subversion), or any set of repos who share a root commit (in a decentralized revision control system like Git)."

Building images within OpenShift adheres to this rule. When performing source builds in OpenShift, the platform will pull source code from a single repository and uses this code to build a single image. When using the source strategy for builds, it is possible to specify individual branches or tags. There is only one codebase per container application. Complex distributed systems containing multiple applications each have their own codebase and will result in multiple container images.

Contrary to this rule it is also possible to specify a *context dir* to extract specific parts of the codebase during a build. This can be used to provide flexibility when migrating existing codebases to OpenShift.

Every developer can check out/clone their own copy of the codebase and may deploy and run it in the OpenShift projects that they create. The codebase is the same across all deploys and is collaboratively shared—albeit with different levels of staged commits—throughout the software delivery lifecycle.

Refer to Chapters 4 and 6 for more information.

Dependencies

"A twelve-factor app never relies on implicit existence of system-wide packages."

In OpenShift, applications are deployed as *immutable* images. These images are created by performing an image build. The built image is "fully contained" in that all software packages that the application is dependent on are contained within the image. Containers by design implicitly support this rule.

Once created, it is considered an *anti-pattern* to add new software and packages at run time to the deployed container. While it is potentially possible to do this, the container reverts back to its immutable image-based state when a container is redeployed or restarted.

During the image build process, explicit addition of software packages that the application is dependent on can be done in a number of ways:

- Declarative dependency management at the source-code level using the relevant tool (e.g., Maven, Ruby Gems, Pip)
- Custom base images used in the build process containing all required dependencies
- Specifying a custom Dockerfile in a BuildConfig when using the Source strategy in an OpenShift source build

Refer to Chapter 6 for more information.

Configuration

"Apps sometimes store config as constants in the code. This is a violation of twelve-factor, which requires strict separation of config from code. Config varies substantially across deploys, code does not."

In general it's considered an anti-pattern to package all environment-dependent information (in properties files, for example) into the immutable image itself. There is nothing explicitly stopping the developer from doing this, but by using the configuration mechanisms available we can separate configuration from code.

As shown in Chapter 5, OpenShift has a number of mechanisms by which application configuration can be managed and injected into a container during the deployment phase (e.g., secrets, configmaps, and environment variables).

However, one refinement that we do recommend is to avoid placing sensitive information into environment variables as they may be visible on the OpenShift console. Secrets are a more suitable mechanism for handling this kind of information.

Refer to Chapter 5 for more information.

Backing Services

"The code for a twelve-factor app makes no distinction between local and third-party services…Each distinct backing service is a resource."

Utilizing the Kubernetes *Services* and *Endpoints* resources is the best approach to abstract local or third-party services. Services can be backed by *pods* running on the platform or may point to other off-platform resources such as a database. Services are DNS resolvable within the platform, thus making them easily discoverable by name. Services are dynamically updated at runtime—for instance, when pods are autoscaled due to load or are replaced as software updates are made available, or when pods are rescheduled onto another node due to node maintenance or eviction.

Refer to Chapters 5 and 3 for more information.

Build, Release, Run

"The twelve-factor app uses strict separation between the build, release, and run stages."

In OpenShift the *Build* stage is the process of assembling all the application source artifacts, building the application container image and pushing the resultant image to the OpenShift Registry.

The *Release* stage is the triggering of new deployments based on configured *image change* triggers within the OpenShift DeploymentConfig resource or by manually performing a deployment via the *CLI* or web console. The DeploymentConfig can receive notifications from the OpenShift Registry about new images being added or image tag changes and react by performing a deployment or redeployment of pods based on those changes.

OpenShift deployment strategies can also handle rollback of pods to the previous version in the case of errors as well as scriptable hooks which can be used to perform actions at the start, middle, or end of the deployment process.

The *Run* stage is handled by the underlying Kubernetes scheduler which schedules a pod to run on a node. Once scheduled, the node executes all the images contained within a pod using the underlying container mechanism (e.g., Docker).

To ensure that traffic isn't sent to a pod before it has fully started, a *readiness probe* can be configured to check the status of the application. Only when the probe completes successfully will traffic be forwarded to the pod.

Pipeline support in OpenShift allows teams to visibly automate tasks within the build release and run stages. Pipeline failures may be remediated quickly by the appropriate teams. Different communication channels (such as web, chat, or email) can be integrated. Complex processes including manual approval steps for promotion of particular builds into environments can be achieved. By allowing teams to automate, test, and continually close the feedback loop, faster and higher quality software releases into production ensue.

Refer to Chapters 4 and 6 for more information.

Processes

"Twelve-factor processes are stateless and share-nothing."

Typically, OpenShift pods contain a single instance of a running application. Multiple container instances share nothing other than a network address space, based on the OpenShift namespace. Storage in pods running on OpenShift is ephemeral—for example, any data written to */tmp* on a pod will be lost when the pod is destroyed.

However, it may not be possible to rewrite or modify existing applications to move to a stateless/share-nothing architecture before deploying them onto OpenShift.

OpenShift has a number of mechanisms that can help with running stateful container-based applications.

Session Affinity

The OpenShift Router supports HTTP session affinity (sticky sessions).

Even though shared HTTP sessions are a violation of the 12 factor rule, you can reliably achieve them in OpenShift if you choose.

OpenShift supports the deployment of JBoss Data Grid to provide a multinode scalable distributed cache. This can be used for storing large data sets as well as HTTP session data if supported by the underlying web frameworks (e.g., JBoss EAP, Spring Cache, etc.).

Storage

OpenShift supports the mounting of shared storage onto pods and have that storage be reattached to the pod in case of a pod restart. This is done via persistent volumes and persistent volume claims.

At the time of writing, OpenShift supports the following file volume types:

- NFS
- HostPath
- GlusterFS
- Ceph RBD
- OpenStack Cinder

- AWS Elastic Block Store (EBS)
- GCE Persistent Disk
- iSCSI
- Fibre Channel

This area is discussed in detail in the OpenShift Container Platform documentation (*https://docs.openshift.com*).

Stateful Pods

StatefulSets are a Kubernetes feature that enables pods to be stopped and restarted while retaining the same network address and storage attached to them. StatefulSets (PetSets in OCP 3.4) are still an experimental feature, but full support should be added in an upcoming release.

Port Binding

"The twelve-factor app is completely self-contained and does not rely on runtime injection of a webserver into the execution environment to create a web-facing service."

OpenShift ships with a HAProxy-based router which provides ingress routing of HTTP/HTTPS traffic into the running pods. While the main use case is to support web traffic, it is also possible to support non-HTTP traffic (e.g., AMQP) by passing the traffic over SSL and adding the route hostname via the *Server Name Indication* (SNI) header. It is also possible to integrate existing load/balancing tiers into Open-Shift.

The *Router* also supports connection rate limiting, metrics, router sharding, and sub-domain wildcards.

For more information, see *http://red.ht/2p2CIdD* and *http://red.ht/2p2LkB9*.

OpenShift Services allow for easy DNS discovery within the platform so that one app may become a backing service for another app. This aggregation and chaining of services is a common pattern in microservices architecture.

Concurrency

"In the twelve-factor app, processes are a first class citizen...The process model truly shines when it comes time to scale out."

The running instantiation of an image is the container. A container in OpenShift is simply a Linux process that has been provided a unique set of capabilities by the host Linux kernel. This particular 12 factor app rule seems written for container application platforms like OpenShift!

The basic scaling model in OpenShift is to scale pods (one or more containers) horizontally either manually or via a configured autoscaler. It is possible to scale vertically in OpenShift but you run the risk of consuming too many resources on a node (e.g., CPU/RAM) and then running into difficulties when the scheduler is unable to schedule the pod or, even worse, the scheduler killing the pod when resources become low on the node.

Critical to the scaling and scheduling aspect of OpenShift is the addition of *Limits* and *Requests* for both CPU and memory resources on the pods.

Kubernetes is declarative. Crashed pods are managed simply by the Replication Controller that keeps the desired number of running pods available at all times. User-initiated restarts and shutdowns are similarly controlled.

For more information, see *http://red.ht/2nFhe5A* or refer to Chapter 7.

Disposability

"The twelve-factor app's processes are disposable, meaning they can be started or stopped at a moment's notice."

Container-based architectures—compared with more traditional VM or bare-metal-based *n*-tier architectures—have a group of specific traits that compare the disposable nature of containers to the uniqueness of virtual or bare-metal machines.

When your application changes—you do not modify the runtime container as you might by adding software to a virtual machine—you simply rebuild the image and redeploy the container based on the new version of the image. When your application configuration changes, you do not change properties files in the container itself; you apply the config and redeploy the same container image. When you move an image through a SDLC, you build, tag, and promote the image and configuration rather than rebuilding and configuration managing a virtual machine environment.

By default, OpenShift caches container images (that it pulls from configured image registries) locally on each node that a pod is scheduled to. In this way, OpenShift can start or stop a container at a moment's notice. Kubernetes is declarative (i.e., you do not tell OpenShift to start an application); instead, you declare the desired state of your application (e.g., the number of pods to run) and the platform takes care of that for you.

The quality of service guarantees described in this 12 factor app rule—robust self-healing, graceful shutdown, minimize startup time—are inherently provided by the Kubernetes orchestration tier within OpenShift.

Replication controller, Scheduler, liveliness, and readiness probes provide for robust self-healing of your container workloads. To help minimize startup times of containers, image layers are cached and distributed to nodes during deployment. A Routing tier coupled with Rolling deployment strategies allow for your business services to be fully available during deployments.

Check out the community Chaos Monkey pod (*http://fabric8.io/guide/chaosMon key.html*) as a way of testing the resilience of your system by randomly killing pods to check that your system behaves properly.

OpenShift also supports idling where the pods can be scaled to zero when there's no traffic being routed to them. For more information, take a look at *http://red.ht/ 2nZbRjD*.

Dev/Prod Parity

"The twelve-factor app is designed for continuous deployment by keeping the gap between development and production small."

OpenShift represents a platform approach that allows your organization to reorganize the delivery of software products by teams that embody cross-cutting concerns (e.g., development, testing, databases, operations, security, business analysis). Teams can be aligned in whatever way makes most sense—for example, they may be aligned to single lines of business within an organization.

Support for deployment strategies and pipelines enables you to configure OpenShift to automate the delivery of container-based applications and so minimize the time gap between development and production.

As a container management platform, OpenShift removes and eases many of the traditional infrastructure provisioning events that typically occur in the delivery of software process. Such provisioning events often slow down, add friction, and help make environments heterogeneous and fragile.

These are some of the elements that, put together, give you the flexibility to prioritize and deploy resources to best ensure that software quickly passes through quality control gates.

Logs

"A twelve-factor app never concerns itself with routing or storage of its output stream."

OpenShift provides "logging as a service" for operational and container application workloads on the platform. Container applications use the STDOUT and STDERR convention to log. In OpenShift, Docker is configured to use the systemd journal daemon. The docker logging driver reads log events directly from the container's output.

This means your applications do not need to configure specific log files and directories within your application. Logs are streamed using *fluentd* to the appropriate log analysis system. By default, this is based on Elasticsearch and Kibana in OpenShift, but it could be an external log aggregator system such as Datadog, Splunk, or Hadoop/Hive.

If using the logging service in OpenShift, RBAC is integrated so you can only see logs for the container applications you have access to. Indexed logs are curated, so that indices may be retained and managed on an ongoing basis to prevent running out of storage. The OpenShift aggregated container log design adheres to this 12 factor app rule and extends its use to operational platform logs as well.

Refer to Chapter 7 for more information.

Admin Processes

"Run admin/management tasks as one-off processes."

OpenShift provides a secure read-eval-print-loop shell (REPL) for all containers that package a shell and libraries to support it. You can access a container's shell console exposed using the OpenShift API, integrated into the web-ui under "Pod", "Terminal", or from the ID or CLI using `oc rsh` commands. Access to the Terminal can be disabled by cluster admins if desired.

Running one-off tasks such as database migrations can be achieved through leveraging OpenShift's deployment hooks to run scripts at multiple stages of a pod deployment's lifecycle. OpenShift deviates from this rule as written, in that containers are immutable. One-off processes that affect the application should interact through either rebuilding and redeploying the container image from a well-known source code version or updating the applied configuration using environment variables, secrets, and configuration maps. Integrated deployment pipeline support in OpenShift makes visible smaller code releases, allowing teams to promote image and configuration through a well-defined software delivery lifecycle.

Security

The initial 12 factors did not mention any aspects of application security. Security is a broad subject spread across multiple tiers and approaches. OpenShift doesn't force any explicit security approach on application developers, and they are free to choose whichever approach suits their needs. However, OpenShift does provide a tiered approach to container security which it enforces at a platform level. The following is an incomplete list of security facilities available within OpenShift:

- Red Hat Enterprise Linux—providing SELinux, Kernel Namespaces, CGroups, and Seccomp security facility.
- Secure private registry, white/black list of third-party external registries.

- Reproducible container builds with image signing and scanning.
- Secured and managed container deployments, pod-level privileges via *Security Context Constraints* which block *root* access by default.
- Network isolation via multi-tenancy plug-in.
- API, console, and web secured via role-based access controls. This can be backed by integration into multiple backends (e.g., LDAP, OAuth, etc.).

Summary

We have listed here the classic "12 factors" of cloud native applications and demonstrated how these *factors* relate to OpenShift. While this has been a technology-centric view, let's conclude by recalling that technology and organizational culture are in a mutually dependent orbit. With OpenShift we are trying to reinforce some desirable target behaviors—collaboration, experimentation—which may come to alter the culture itself.

But for sustainable change, bottom-up grassroots support needs to be matched from the top-down. For those benefits to be enduring—software changes delivered faster, cheaper, materially impacting users—organizational, people, and cultural issues must also be attended to.

Index

About the Authors

Stefano Picozzi is the Red Hat lead in OpenShift for Australia and New Zealand. He has been helping clients transform to take advantage of container management platforms since OpenShift's general availability in 2012. His background includes management and advisory in software process improvement and cloud infrastructure solutions to large enterprises across the Asia Pacific region.

Mike Hepburn has a background in application architecture, middleware integration and operations, development, and helping large organizations continually transform and adapt to the ever-changing IT landscape. He is currently Red Hat's ANZ PaaS subject matter expert.

Noel O'Connor is a Principal Consultant and Architect at Red Hat. He has extensive experience leading and delivering key customer projects for Red Hat customers around the world. He's the founder of the Sydney Kubernetes Meetup and is passionate about helping organizations across Europe and Asia as a navigator on their OpenShift journey to containerization and PaaS.

Colophon

The animal on the cover of *DevOps with OpenShift* is the white-bellied parrot (*Pionites leucogaster*), also known as the green-thighed parrot. Making its home in the forests of the Amazon basin in Brazil, the white-bellied parrot is a small, colorful bird with a yellow or orange head, white underside, and green wings.

White-bellied parrots feed on a variety of fruits and seeds. They nest in tree hollows high off the ground to avoid predators. Some are kept as pets, and they can be trained to imitate sounds like whistles and bells, although they cannot imitate speech like other parrots.

The population of the white-bellied parrot is expected to decline significantly over the next few decades due to the rapid deforestation taking place in the Amazon basin. Because of this the species is currently listed as endangered.

Many of the animals on O'Reilly covers are endangered; all of them are important to the world. To learn more about how you can help, go to *animals.oreilly.com*.

The cover image is from *Buffon*. The cover fonts are URW Typewriter and Guardian Sans. The text font is Adobe Minion Pro; the heading font is Adobe Myriad Condensed; and the code font is Dalton Maag's Ubuntu Mono.

Learn from experts.
Find the answers you need.

Sign up for a **10-day free trial** to get **unlimited access** to all of the content on Safari, including Learning Paths, interactive tutorials, and curated playlists that draw from thousands of ebooks and training videos on a wide range of topics, including data, design, DevOps, management, business—and much more.

Start your free trial at:

oreilly.com/safari

(No credit card required.)

Milton Keynes UK
Ingram Content Group UK Ltd.
UKHW051830030924
447839UK00007B/192